LUGHNASADH

Llewellyn's Sabbat Essentials

LUGHNASADH

Rituals, Recipes & Lore for Lammas

Llewellyn Publications
Woodbury, Minnesota

FIRST EDITION
Thirteenth Printing, 2023

Book design by Donna Burch-Brown
Cover art: iStockphoto.com/18232461/©Electric_Crayon,
            iStockphoto.com/24907932©Jane_Kelly,
            iStockphoto.com/19034979/©PixelEmbargo,
            iStockphoto.com/6174373/©shaneillustration
Cover design by Kevin R. Brown
Editing by Laura Graves
Interior illustrations by Mickie Mueller

Llewellyn Publications is a registered trademark of Llewellyn Worldwide Ltd.

Library of Congress Cataloging-in-Publication Data
Marquis, Melanie, 1976–
  Lughnasadh : rituals, recipes & lore for Lammas / Melanie Marquis. —
First edition.
      pages   cm. — (Llewellyn's sabbat essentials)
  Includes bibliographical references and index.
  ISBN 978-0-7387-4178-9
1. Lammas. 2. Witchcraft. I. Title.
  BF1572.L35M37 2015
  299'.94—dc23

                                                                2014048978

Llewellyn Worldwide Ltd. does not participate in, endorse, or have any authority or responsibility concerning private business transactions between our authors and the public.

  All mail addressed to the author is forwarded but the publisher cannot, unless specifically instructed by the author, give out an address or phone number.

  Any Internet references contained in this work are current at publication time, but the publisher cannot guarantee that a specific location will continue to be maintained. Please refer to the publisher's website for links to authors' websites and other sources.

Llewellyn Publications
A Division of Llewellyn Worldwide Ltd.
2143 Wooddale Drive
Woodbury, MN 55125-2989
www.llewellyn.com

Printed in the United States of America

Contents

SERIES INTRODUCTION . . . I

Old Ways . . . 13

New Ways . . . 39

Spells and Divination . . . 69

Recipes and Crafts . . . 93

Prayers and Invocations . . . 129

Rituals of Celebration . . . 147

CORRESPONDENCES FOR LUGHNASADH . . . 175

BIBLIOGRAPHY . . . 189

FURTHER READING . . . 199

INDEX . . . 201

...tion, introspection, discernment, sacrifice, excellent time for magic... ...ty, abundance, strength, growth, protection, honoring ancestors, ...nsformation, or communicating with the dead, sacred wells, hot... ...s for magick, astronomical midpoint between the Summer Sol... ...at 15 degrees Leo in the Northern Hemisphere, Sun at... ...uarius in the Southern Hemisphere, Mother Goddess, Earth... ...Goddess, water nymphs, tree nymphs, the spirit of the land, ...Earth God, Solar God, the warrior, the protector, the sac... ...he dying god, the spirit of vegetation, the newly crowned king, ...Dryads, Demeter, Kore, Zwannotar, Nemesis, Ops, Ha... ...Juturna, Stata Mater, Danu, Artemis, Ceres, Lug... ...cultilte, Consus, Thor, Vulcan, Thoth, Lobt, Vertumnus, ...ar energies, happiness, transformation. Brown: Earth energies, ...llumination, success, divine power, harvest. Green: Abundance ...t, vegetation Herb Blackberry: Protection, binding, defense, ab... ...healing, abundance, friendship, love Allspice: Money, wealth, ...nagickal power Basil: Protection, luck, love, wealth, abundance ...Solar energies, healing, protection, friendship, peace, prosperit...

LLEWELLYN'S SABBAT ESSENTIALS

LEWELLYN'S SABBAT ESSENTIALS provide instruction and inspiration for honoring each of the modern witch's sabbats. Packed with spells, rituals, meditations, history, lore, invocations, divination, recipes, crafts, and more, each book in this eight-volume series explores both the old and new ways of celebrating the seasonal rites that act as cornerstones in the witch's year.

There are eight sabbats, or holidays, celebrated by Wiccans and many other Neopagans (modern Pagans) today. Together, these eight sacred days make up what's known as the Wheel of the Year, or the sabbat cycle, with each sabbat corresponding to an important turning point in nature's annual journey through the seasons.

Devoting our attention to the Wheel of the Year allows us to better attune ourselves to the energetic cycles of nature and listen to what each season is whispering (or shouting!) to us, rather than working against the natural tides. What better time to start new projects than as the earth reawakens after a long winter, and suddenly everything is blooming and growing and shooting up out of the ground again? And what better time to meditate and plan ahead than during the introspective slumber of winter? With Llewellyn's Sabbat Essentials, you'll learn how to focus on the spiritual aspects of the Wheel of the Year, how to move through it and with it in harmony, and how to celebrate your own ongoing growth and achievements. This may be your first book on Wicca, Witchcraft, or Paganism, or your newest addition to a bookcase or e-reader already crammed with magical wisdom. In either case, we hope you will find something of value here to take with you on your journey.

Take a Trip Through the Wheel of the Year

The eight sabbats each mark an important point in nature's annual cycles. They are depicted as eight evenly spaced spokes on a wheel representing the year as a whole; the dates on which they fall are nearly evenly spaced on the calendar, as well.

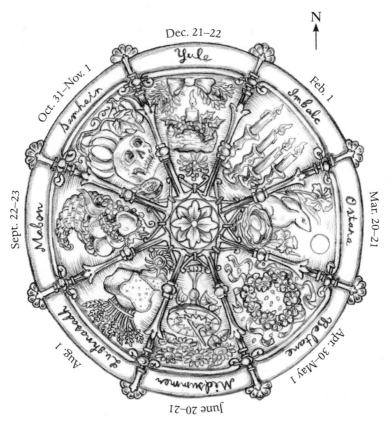

N

Dec. 21–22

Yule

Feb. 1

Imbolc

Oct. 31–Nov. 1

Samhain

Mar. 20–21

Ostara

Sept. 22–23

Mabon

Apr. 30–May 1

Beltane

Aug. 1

Lughnasadh

Midsummer

June 20–21

Wheel of the Year—Northern Hemisphere
(All solstice and equinox dates are approximate,
and one should consult an almanac or a calendar
to find the correct dates each year.)

3
......

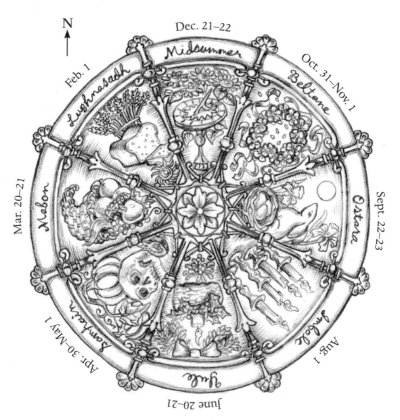

Dec. 21–22

Midsummer

Oct. 31–Nov. 1

Beltane

Feb. 1

Lughnasadh

Mar. 20–21

Mabon

Sept. 22–23

Ostara

Apr. 30–May 1

Samhain

Aug. 1

Imbolc

Yule

June 20–21

Wheel of the Year—Southern Hemisphere

The wheel is comprised of two groups of four holidays each. There are four solar festivals relating to the sun's position in the sky, dividing the year into quarters: the Spring Equinox, the Summer Solstice, the Fall Equinox, and the Winter Solstice, all of which are dated astronomically and thus vary slightly from year to year. Falling in between these quarter days are the cross-quarter holidays, or fire festivals: Imbolc, Beltane, Lughnasadh, and Samhain. The quarters are sometimes called the Lesser Sabbats and the cross-quarters the Greater Sabbats, although neither cycle is "superior" to the other. In the Southern Hemisphere seasons are opposite those in the north, and the sabbats are consequently celebrated at different times.

While the book you are holding only focuses on Lughnasadh, it can be helpful to know how it fits in with the cycle as a whole.

The Winter Solstice, also called Yule or Midwinter, occurs when nighttime has reached its maximum length; after the solstice, the length of the days will begin to increase. Though the cold darkness is upon us, there is a promise of brighter days to come. In Wiccan lore, this is the time when the young solar god is born. In some Neopagan traditions, this is when the Holly King is destined to lose the battle to his lighter aspect the Oak King. Candles are lit, feasts are enjoyed, and evergreen foliage is brought in the house as a reminder that, despite the harshness of winter, light and life have endured.

At Imbolc (also spelled Imbolg), the ground is just starting to thaw, signaling that it's time to start preparing the fields for the approaching sowing season. We begin to awaken from our months of introspection and start to sort out what we have learned over that time, while also taking the first steps to make plans for our future. Some Wiccans also bless candles at Imbolc, another symbolic way of coaxing along the now perceptibly stronger light.

On the Spring Equinox, also known as Ostara, night and day are again equal in length, and following this, the days will grow longer than the nights. The Spring Equinox is a time of renewal, a time to plant seeds as the earth once again comes to life. We decorate eggs as a symbol of hope, life, and fertility, and we perform rituals to energize ourselves so that we can find the power and passion to live and grow.

In agricultural societies, Beltane marked the start of the summer season. Livestock were led out to graze in abundant pastures and trees burst into beautiful and fragrant blossom. Rituals were performed to protect crops, livestock, and people. Fires were lit and offerings were made in the hopes of gaining divine protection. In Wiccan mythos, the young goddess is impregnated by the young god. We all have something we want to harvest by the end of the year—plans we are determined to realize—and Beltane is a great time to enthusiastically get that process in full swing.

The Summer Solstice is the longest day of the year. It's also called Litha, or Midsummer. Solar energies are at their apex, and the power of Nature is at its height. In Wiccan lore, it's the time when the solar god's power is at its greatest (so, paradoxically, his power must now start to decrease), having impregnated the maiden goddess, who then transforms into the earth mother. In some Neopagan traditions, this is when the Holly King once again battles his lighter aspect, this time vanquishing the Oak King. It's generally a time of great merriment and celebration.

At Lughnasadh, the major harvest of the summer has ripened. Celebrations are held, games are played, gratitude is expressed, and feasts are enjoyed. Also known as Lammas, this is the time we celebrate the first harvest—whether that means the first of our garden crops or the first of our plans that have come to fruition. To celebrate the grain harvest, bread is often baked on this day.

The Autumn Equinox, also called Mabon, marks another important seasonal change and a second harvest. The sun shines equally on both hemispheres, and the lengths of night and day are equal. After this point, the nights will again be longer than the days. In connection with the harvest, the day is celebrated as a festival of sacrifice and of the dying god, and tribute is paid to the sun and the fertile earth.

To the Celtic people, Samhain marked the start of the winter season. It was the time when the livestock was slaughtered and the final harvest was gathered before the inevitable plunge into the depths of winter's darkness. Fires were lit to help wandering spirits on their way, and offerings were given in the names of the gods and the ancestors. Seen as a beginning,

Samhain is now often called the Witches' New Year. We honor our ancestors, wind down our activities, and get ready for the months of introspection ahead ... and the cycle continues.

The Modern Pagan's Relationship to the Wheel

Modern Pagans take inspiration from many pre-Christian spiritual traditions, exemplified by the Wheel of the Year. The cycle of eight festivals we recognize throughout modern Pagandom today was never celebrated in full by any one particular pre-Christian culture. In the 1940s and 1950s a British man named Gerald Gardner created the new religion of Wicca by drawing on a variety of cultures and traditions, deriving and adapting practices from pre-Christian religion, animistic beliefs, folk magick, and various shamanic disciplines and esoteric orders. He combined multicultural equinox and solstice traditions with Celtic feast days and early European agricultural and pastoral celebrations to create a single model that became the framework for the Wiccan ritual year.

This Wiccan ritual year is popularly followed by Wiccans and witches, as well as many eclectic Pagans of various stripes. Some Pagans only observe half of the sabbats, either the quarters or the cross-quarters. Other Pagans reject the Wheel of the Year altogether and follow a festival calendar based on the culture of whatever specific path they follow rather than a nature-based agrarian cycle. We all have such unique paths in Paganism that it is important not to make any assumptions about another's based on your own; maintaining an open and positive attitude is what makes the Pagan community thrive.

Many Pagans localize the Wheel of the Year to their own environment. Wicca has grown to become a truly global religion, but few of us live in a climate mirroring Wicca's British Isles origins. While traditionally Imbolc is the beginning of the thaw and the awakening of the earth, it is the height of winter in many northern climes. While Lammas may be a grateful celebration of the harvest for some, in areas prone to drought and forest fires it is a dangerous and uncertain time of year.

There are also the two hemispheres to consider. While it's winter in the Northern Hemisphere, it's summer in the Southern Hemisphere. While Pagans in America are celebrating Yule and the Winter Solstice, Pagans in Australia are celebrating Midsummer. The practitioner's own lived experiences are more important than any dogma written in a book when it comes to observing the sabbats.

In that spirit, you may wish to delay or move up celebrations so that the seasonal correspondences better fit your own locale, or you may emphasize different themes for each sabbat as you experience it. This series should make such options easily accessible to you.

No matter what kind of place you live on the globe, be it urban, rural, or suburban, you can adapt sabbat traditions and practices to suit your own life and environment. Nature is all around us; no matter how hard we humans try to insulate ourselves from nature's cycles, these recurring seasonal changes are inescapable. Instead of swimming against the tide, many modern Pagans embrace each season's unique energies, whether dark, light, or in between, and integrate these energies into aspects of our own everyday lives.

Llewellyn's Sabbat Essentials offer all the information you need in order to do just that. Each book will resemble the one you hold in your hands. The first chapter, *Old Ways*, shares the history and lore that have been passed down, from mythology and pre-Christian traditions to any vestiges still seen in modern life. *New Ways* then spins those themes and elements into the manners in which modern Pagans observe and celebrate the sabbat. The next chapter focuses on *Spells and Divination* appropriate to the season or based in folklore, while the following one, *Recipes and Crafts*, offers ideas for decorating your home, hands-on crafts, and recipes that take advantage of seasonal offerings. The chapter on *Invocations and Meditations* provides ready-made calls and prayers you may use in ritual, meditation, or journaling. The *Rituals and Celebrations* chapter provides three complete rituals: one for a solitary, one for two people, and one for a whole group such as a coven, circle, or grove. (Feel free to adapt each or any ritual to your own needs, substituting your own offerings, calls, invocations, magical workings, and so on. When planning a group ritual, try to be conscious of any special needs participants may have. There are many wonderful books available that delve into the fine points of facilitating ritual if you don't have experience in this department.) Finally, in the back of the book you'll find a complete list of correspondences for the holiday, from magical themes to deities to foods, colors, symbols, and more.

By the end of this book you'll have the knowledge and the inspiration to celebrate the sabbat with gusto. By honoring the Wheel of the Year, we reaffirm our connection to nature so that as her endless cycles turn, we're able to go with the flow and enjoy the ride.

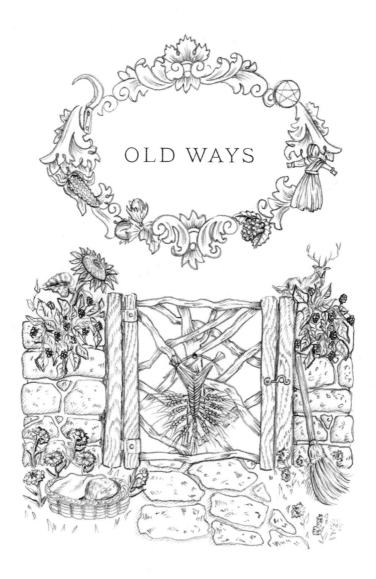

OLD WAYS

on, introspection, discernment, sacrifice, excellent time for magic

, abundance, strength, growth, protection, honoring ancestors,

formation, or communications with the dead, sacred wells, hill

for magick, astronomical midpoint between the Summer Sols

at 15 degrees Leo in the Northern Hemisphere, Sun at

arius in the Southern Hemisphere, Mother Goddess, Earth

Goddess, water nymphs, tree nymphs, the spirit of the land, t

Earth God, Solar God, the warrior, the protector, the sacr

dying god, the spirit of vegetation, the newly crowned king,

Dryads, Demeter, Kore, Luannotar, Nemesis, Ops, Vult

Juturna, Stata Mater, Danu, Artemis, Ceres, Lug

tle, Consus, Thor, Vulcan, Thoth, Loki, Vertumnus,

energies, happiness, transformation. Brown: Earth energies,

lumination, success, divine power, harvest Green: Abundance,

vegetation Herb Blackberry: Protection, binding, defense, clu

healing, abundance, friendship, love Allspice: Money, wealth,

magical power Basil: Protection, luck, love, wealth, abundance,

Solar energies, healing, protection, friendship, peace, prosperi

LUGHNASADH (PRONOUNCED *LOO-nah-sah*) is the first of three harvest celebrations in the Pagan Wheel of the Year. It is typically held from sundown on July 31 through sundown on August 1, though some celebrate on or around August 5 or 6, referred to as "Old Lammas" or "Old Style Lammas." The festival can also be timed astrologically to coincide with the point where Leo reaches 15 degrees relative to the position of the sun. Agricultural timing is also an option, as Lughnasadh might be celebrated as the first fruits of the harvest begin to ripen in your own garden or regional farmlands. In Ireland the first of August was celebrated as Lugnasad, and in Scotland it was called Lunasda or Lunasdal. In the Isle of Man the day was called Luanistyn, and in Wales the day was celebrated as the Gwyl Awst, or Feast of Augustus. In England it was called Lammas, a derivation of the Old English *hlafmaesse*, literally "loaf-mass."

Originating in Ireland, Lughnasadh (or Lugnasad) gets its name from the Celtic deity Lugh (pronounced *LOO*), some-times spelled Lug. In modern times, Lugh is often thought of as a solar deity and harvest god, but originally he seems to have been understood as a god of human skill, kings, and a patron of heroes (Hutton, 327). Lugh was king of the *Tuatha de Danaan*, a race of divine beings whose name translates as "people of the goddess Danu." Danu was a mother goddess associated with water, the earth, fertility, and victory. With the help of Lugh, Danu's followers managed to displace the Fir Bolg and Fomoiri, the previous caste of divine rulers who were portrayed in Irish myths as monstrous beings. Lugh was attributed with great skill in craft and warfare, and over time, he became equated to the Roman god Mercury (Futrell, 105).

In *The Festival of Lughnasa*, Mary MacNeill's comprehensive study of traditional Celtic Lughnasadh customs, the author concluded that the festival most likely originally consisted of a mix of ceremony, feasting, and ritual theatrics, usually held on hilltops or waterside. There was likely, according to the author, a ritual in which the first fruit from the grain harvest would be brought to the top of a hill and buried as an offering. The author also reports as common practice a bull sacrifice and ceremony involving the animal's hide, as well as a ritual play retelling Lugh's triumph over blight or famine, in which a human head was installed on top of a hill by a person playing the role of Lugh. This was followed by three days of festivities. According to MacNeill, feasting on bilberries, sacrificial bull flesh, and the new food of the predominant crop of the harvest (grains in early days and potatoes in latter years) served as a primary aspect of the celebrations (Hutton, 327–328).

While our knowledge of early Lughnasadh celebrations is decidedly limited, the elements we do know of are amply intriguing. One curious aspect of this sort is the fact that Lughnasadh is sometimes referred to as Lugh's wedding feast. This idea stems from a reference in a fifteenth-century version of the *Tochmarc Emire*, a medieval Irish saga. The manuscript makes reference to Lugh's *banais rigi*, or kingship wedding feast. Although the manuscript does not make specific mention of Lugh's actual mating with anyone in particular, Ireland indeed had a long tradition of tying kingship to union with a goddess figure. Kingship was often legitimized through marriage to a woman of royal lineage, and as such women were often associated with goddesses and may have been seen as priestesses of the goddess or embodiments thereof. Literary descriptions of such kingship wedding feasts typically involve a sexual element and the administering of a special drink by the "goddess" to the new king. Lugh's kingship wedding feast might be understood as symbolic of a coronation: he is united with the goddess—the land—and his rule over it is legitimized through the process (Talcroft, 26–28).

More commonly, however, Lughnasadh is referred to not as a wedding feast but as Lugh's funeral games held in honor of his stepmother Tailtiu (pronounced TAL-chi-uh). Tailtiu was the wife of the last king of the Fir Bolg. When the Fir Bolg were overthrown, Tailtiu remarried to one of the new ruling class, the Tuatha de Danaan (Roy, 254). According to legend, Tailtiu died of exhaustion after clearing the fields of Ireland for agriculture, and Lugh initiated the Fair of Tailteann in her honor as a wake fair including feasting, games, and sports. Whether or not the games were actually the inspiration of Lugh himself must remain a mystery, but we do know as fact that an event called the Fair of Tailteann was held annually on the first of August at a locality midway between Navan and Kells, near a reputed gravesite of the legendary Tailtiu in what is now County Meath, Ireland (Joyce, 438). Dating back to at least the sixth century, the fair drew together people from throughout Ireland and Scotland (Roy, 253). Popular for its athletic games, a report from the fair written in 1169 records that the horses and chariots alone who gathered to witness the spectacle stretched in a line more than six miles long (Joyce, 439). Competitive sports weren't the only entertainments at the Fair of Tailteann, which later became known as Telltown on the Blackwater. It was also a time of romance, when partnerships were arranged between available youths and ceremonies to formalize the new unions were often performed on the spot (Joyce, 438–441).

Lughnasadh was a popular time for trial marriages, which were temporary partnerships that lasted for a year and a day until the end of the next fair at which time the union could be dissolved if so desired. Such partnerships are sometimes called Telltown marriages. Handfasts (a type of Pagan marriage ceremony) were quite common at Lughnasadh, with more permanent unions forged in addition to the temporary trial ones. The couple being handfasted would gather witnesses, clasp their right hands together, and exchange vows of devotion to one another. Gifts were often exchanged between the spouses, taking a variety of forms, from rings and gold coins to red ribbons, gloves, and silver toothpicks (Thompson).

Though arguably the most famous, the Fair of Tailteann was by no means the only August fair known in Ireland. A similar fair was held at Carman, in what is now County Kildare. Local legend relates that Carman was the name of the mother of an invading force who threatened Ireland. According to lore, Carman gave up her life and died a hostage as a way to guarantee that the invaders would not return. Giving credence to the tale, archeologists discovered near the site the remains of a young woman who seems to have been buried alive (Roy, 254). It may seem odd to us to have a fair near a grave site, but such locations seem to have been preferred. The Lughnasadh fairs were typically held near the burial mounds of mythical, divine female heroes such as Tailtiu or Carman. An old poem

that speaks of the fair of Carman does well to illustrate the
significance and appeal:

> *The renowned field is the cemetary of kings,*
> *The dearly loved of nobles grades;*
> *There are many meeting mounds,*
> *For their ever loved ancestral hosts.*
> *To mourn for queens and for kings,*
> *To denounce aggression and tyranny,*
> *Often were the fair hosts in autumn*
> *Upon the smooth brow of noble old Carman.*
>
> (O'Curry and Sullivan, 530)

Seven races were held on each of the days of the fair at Carman, with the final day reserved for horse races and other
equine contests. There was a food and clothing market, a
livestock market, and a market dedicated to the sell of exotic
goods and the trade of foreign gold and silver. Matters of laws
and rights for the province were considered and settled during
the fair, as well (ibid.).

Such fairs were in fact quite common in Ireland. In Leinster, a great fair was held once every three years, beginning
at Lughnasadh and ending on the sixth of August. A poem in
the Book of Leinster, written around the year 1000, warns that
early grayness, balding, misrule, and other misfortunes might

befall those who neglect to hold the fair once every three years, as tradition decreed proper. On the other hand, if the fair were held regularly, the poem promises, the people could expect blessings of abundance and prosperity in the form of corn, milk, fruit, fish, and other types of good fortune. The fair in Leinster brought together people of many districts, with the chiefs or sub-kings of various provinces far and wide coming out to the six-day celebration. Games and competition were the chief occupations at the fair, with contests held for horse riding, chariot racing, competition between nobles, special games for women, and more (Joyce, 438–441). The Lughnasadh fairs often kept a generally serious and formal tone; women and men were sometimes separated into different areas of the fairgrounds to promote morality and help reduce the chances of spontaneous orgies (Roy, 253–254).

For those who couldn't make the fairs, there were plenty of other ways to celebrate. Protection magick, for example, was widely practiced. Horses and cattle were driven to walk through water as a means of purifying the animals and blessing them, as rivers and other water sources were considered sacred by the Irish, especially at the time of Lughnasadh. Other prominent customs involved the first fruits of the harvest, which would be either offered to divine spirits or ceremonially eaten. Potluck-style feasting was a big part of the celebrations, and often the feasts included dancing as well as exhibitions of performance combat. Symbols of fertility and abundance, flower garlands were hung as decoration and were also worn on the bodies of Lughnasadh revelers (Futrell, 104–105).

Another name for Lugnasadh in Ireland was Bron-trogain. *Bron* meant bringing forth, and *trogain* meant the earth or ground, so "Bron-trogain" represented the bringing forth of the fruits of the earth—in other words, the harvest. Bron also signified the idea of sorrow or distress, giving the name Bron-trogain another layer of mystery and meaning. There's a line in an old Irish tale called the "Wooing of Emer" that says of Bron-trogain, "It is then the earth sorrows under [the weight of] its fruit" (Joyce, 389).

In the second half of the fifth century, Germanic tribes from south of Denmark and Germany began migrating into parts of Britain, establishing what came to be known as the Anglo-Saxon culture. As the newcomers adapted to the local customs and local climate, traditions inevitably blended and changed. Perhaps influenced by the Celtic Lughnasadh, the Germanic tribes who migrated into Britain began celebrating at the start of August the holiday of *hlafmaesse*, which translates as "loaf mass," a celebration of the first fruits of the wheat harvest. Harvest rituals and customs were not unknown in the early history of Germany and Denmark, but it wasn't until the Anglo-Saxons established their culture in Britain that they began holding a harvest celebration around the start of August. Originally, hlafmaesse was dedicated to Pagan deities, but as the Germanic people converted to Christianity, hlafmaesse was absorbed into the rites of the church as a Feast of First Fruits, a day on which bread would be baked from the first grains of the harvest and carried to the church to be blessed and consecrated (Lipkowitz, 227). One traditional Anglo-Saxon Lammas custom was to bake a loaf of hallowed bread, marked on the top with the sign of the cross. The loaf was broken into four pieces, and the four pieces were subsequently crumbled in each of the four corners of the barn, the charm intended to invite blessings and ensure magickal protection (Gomme).

As Anglo-Saxon culture began to more heavily influence Celtic religion, Lammas customs blended with, absorbed, and sometimes replaced, older Lughnasadh traditions, making it rather difficult to discern the exact origins of many practices related to the early August harvest celebrations. When surveying August sabbat traditions throughout the UK, we often find elements of both the Celtic Lughnasadh and the Anglo-Saxon Lammas meshed together, as might be expected. Just as we modern Pagans celebrate the sabbat with a blending of traditions, so too did generations of the past combine the beliefs and practices of different cultures to create rites and rituals fitting for their own time, place, and people.

Despite the fact that the Celtic lands eventually became heavily steeped in Christianity, the Pagan tradition of early August fairs carried on, and Lammastide continued to be celebrated with public feasting and festivity. These fairs generally had an agricultural or harvest theme. One fair that got its start by church decree in 1257 in Highworth, Wiltshire, became famous as one of the biggest cattle markets in the region. The Christians also chose to keep with traditional Pagan symbolism in associating various agricultural saints with the time of the August sabbat. Saint Sidwell, a saint associated with agriculture, is celebrated around the start of August; July 31, August 2, or August 3 are all considered acceptable dates for celebration. Saint Oswald, the patron saint of shepherds and sheep, is honored on August 5 (Groom).

In the Scottish Highlands, the beginning of August marked a time to renew and refresh magickal protections on the crops, livestock, and other property. Rowan crosses were placed over doors as a means of magickal protection, and tar was sometimes painted onto the ears and tails of the livestock in hopes of ensuring their health and safety. Red or blue threads would often be tied onto the cow's tails and magickal charms would be spoken over the udders to help ensure a plentiful milk supply. A ball of cow hair might be placed inside a milk pail to the same effect (Hutton). Special cakes were made for Lughnasadh, called *bonnach Lunastain*, or the Lammas bannock.

The cakes were eaten outdoors, often in fields or valleys. A ritual always accompanied the practice. As the cakes were eaten, small pieces would also be thrown over the shoulders, alternating from left to right. These bits of cake were given as an offering to the fox, the eagle, and other predatory animals, and as each piece was tossed, a plea for the named beast to spare one's livestock was uttered. Similar cake rituals were performed at Beltane, Samhain, and Imbolc as well (Carmichael, 209). In most areas of Scotland, August celebrations were individual and low-key, although in some localities, the customs were more elaborate and communal (Hutton).

A Scottish journal published in 1792 describes one such community-wide custom popular towards the middle of the eighteenth century in Midlothian, an area that borders the city of Edinburgh. Near the beginning of summer, district residents would organize themselves into bands, sometimes numbering upwards of a hundred people per group. By the time Lammas rolled around, it was expected for each band to have finished construction of a special tower. The towers measured about 4 feet in diameter and rarely rose more than 7 or 8 feet in height. Built from squares of sod and sometimes stones, the towers were usually square rather than round in shape, fashioned so that a hole was left in the center to accommodate the insertion of a flagpole. Each band would have their own flag, to be proudly displayed on Lammas morning. It was considered a great disgrace to have one's tower defaced, so the bands kept a close eye on their nearby fellows. If a neighboring band approached, the tower party would bravely meet them, using intimidation and sometimes actual physical fighting to get the threatening group to submit. At midday, the bands would all march to the main village, where they would be met with the accolades of the larger community. Three races were held, and participants vied for the win—prizes included a bonnet embellished with ribbon that was to be placed atop a tall pole, a pair of garters, and a knife (Gomme, i).

To the fishermen of Orkney, Scotland, Lammas meant the end of the more perilous work of the summer season. It was tradition among the fishermen to gather for a final toast at Lammas, asking the higher powers to open the mouths of the fish and to protect the corn (Guthrie, 175).

In Lewis, in the Outer Hebrides, a group of islands off the coast of Scotland, the villagers used to perform a nighttime Lughnasadh ritual in honor of Seonaidh, a water spirit believed to dwell in the sea.

According to Martin Martin, a Scottish writer who died in 1718, each family contributed a bag of malt, and the combined provisions were brewed into ale. One person would be chosen to wade out into the ocean until they were waist-deep, carrying with them a cup of the ale held high. The person would then call out:

*"Seonaidh, I give thee this cup of ale, hoping that thou wilt be
so good as to send us plenty of seaware for enriching
our ground during the coming year."*

The cup of ale was then tossed into the sea, the ritual believed to help ensure a healthy crop in the next growing season by securing an ample supply of "seaware"—a coarse seaweed that was used as fertilizer. The party would then retire to the church, where vigil was kept around a burning candle. At a signal, the candle was extinguished and the villagers would then go out into the fields for a night of cheerful ale drinking (Thompson).

Another custom practiced in parts of Scotland as well as in the north of England was to fashion the last sheaves of corn harvested into a doll, thereafter called a "kirn (corn) baby" or "kirn maiden." These "kirn babies" likely evolved into the familiar corn dollies, first mentioned in England in 1598. Sometimes, the individual that cut the last of the corn would do so blindfolded. After the corn doll was made, it was kept as a magical charm thought to bring good luck to people, property, and livestock (ibid.).

In the Lanark area and a handful of other places in Scotland, one curious Lammas custom called the Riding of the Marches was practiced. It was customary for the magistrates, burgesses, and freemen to make an annual ride around the borders of their territories, which were marked with a series of stones called march stones. The procession of riders checked the march stones one by one to make sure they were all still in their rightful places, and an official report of the findings was written up, signed by witnesses, and filed with the appropriate official (Guthrie, 90–91). One of the march stones was placed in the river, and newcomers to the ride were dunked into the flowing water as a means of initiation (ibid.).

Drums were played while the procession rode, and new march stones were strategically placed wherever boundary lines were found to be unclear. Broom was placed on the hats and drums of the participants, and whenever a new stone had to be erected, a mock battle was held, members of the procession pitted against one another in a display of combat until their rather fragile broom weapons inevitably failed and the group departed in good spirits (ibid., 59–61).

In some localities where boundary marches were held, the young boys of the area would cut down birch boughs and carry these to a central place of assembly, keeping up a spirit of boisterousness and merrymaking along the way (ibid., 79). In Linlithgow, the boundary-marking procession was preceeded by a toast to the sovereign, after which the cups used would be thrown to the assembled crowd. The Linlithgow procession was colorful and elaborate, including carriages and bands of tradespeople bearing banners. Farm workers brought up the rear of the procession, mounted on horseback and wearing bonnets decorated with large quantities of ribbons (Guthrie, 79).

In a journal article from August 1882, G. Lawerence Gomme makes mention of an early Lammastide custom of Anglo-Saxon origins whose echoes were still discernible in some parts of England and Scotland at the time of his writing. During the agricultural growing season, lands were divided into separate tracts and considered to be private property. Lammastide signaled that the growing season was at a close, and in some places, any crops left unharvested or hay that hadn't been picked up by this time were fair game for anyone who made the effort to collect them, regardless of whose charge the land was under.

At Lammastide, fences were removed and private crop lands became common areas of open pasture, free for anyone in the community to use. These pastures were sometimes called "Lammas lands" (Gomme).

Lammas also marked a time when rents were due and tithes were paid. (Knowlson) In England, this tithe was called "Peter's Pence" and demanded that one penny for every house in the country be paid to the church officials. The earliest mention of the tax comes from a letter from Rome written in 1031 to the English clergy. Under Pope Adrian, the tax was extended to Ireland as well (Addis and Arnold, 656–657).

In Wales, Gwyl Awst was celebrated with picnics on hill-tops and community fairs, as well as with other customs common to Celtic festivities held at the time of early August. One such tradition practiced in Wales was to dedicate the first ear of corn harvested to the god Lugh, then bury it on a hilltop. The people would enjoy a feast, then return to the site of the buried corn where they enjoyed a dramatic reenactment of Lugh's triumph over famine. As was common in other parts of the Celtic world, the Welsh celebrations also included games and sporting competitions, singing, dancing, and the forging of marriage arrangements (Roy, 251–253).

Similar harvest festivals are found throughout the world. While timing of such festivals differs from place to place to coincide with local growing seasons, certain elements of such festivals parallel one another so strongly it becomes reasonable to consider that celebrating the various stages of harvest may be a natural human need and cultural tendency that demands expression regardless of time, place, or people.

Consider the rites of the Hopi tribe of the southwestern United States, for example, who marked August with many special harvest rites and rituals. The Marua Dance, also called the Water Moon Dance or Growing Moon Dance, was performed each August in hopes of ensuring human fertility, good weather, and a bountiful harvest. The dancers (all women) carried full stalks of corn, roots and ears still attached, and the leader of the group carried a decorated prayer stick called a *baho*. It was believed that the prayers inscribed on the baho could be observed and deciphered by Muingwa, god of fertility and germination. Prayers were made to the deity in hopes of procuring a good harvest and ensuring fertile ground for the next planting season. The Snake Dance was performed the third week of August. The Hopi villagers would go out for four days collecting snakes, traveling to the north, east, south, and west to gather up these creatures that were considered sacred to Tawa, a deity associated with the sun. The snakes were brought back to the village and incorporated into a ritual dance intended to protect the harvest and secure an adequate supply of rain (Eaton, 63–67). Though Hopi harvest rites emerged completely independent of Celtic harvest rites, these very different cultural traditions nevertheless share common themes of gratitude, hope, sacrifice, and harvest.

Harvest festivals were held by indigenous people from the Southeastern US, as well. The Cherokee, Creek, Choctaw, and Chickasaw tribes celebrated the first of the corn harvest with a ceremony known as the Green Corn Festival. Specific dates for celebrating the occasion differed, as the festival was timed to coincide with the ripening of the first ears of corn. It could be held as early as spring and as late as late summer, but most tribes celebrated sometime between July and August. People from surrounding villages would gather in fellowship to celebrate the harvest and remember the sacredness of life. It was a time of renewal: conflicts were settled, debts and arguments were forgiven, and an atmosphere of peace prevailed. Festivities included singing, dancing, and discussions of moral and ethical topics. Offerings were made to the gods in a spirit of thanksgiving, and a feast was often enjoyed (Cooke).

Harvest festivals are also common in Africa. In parts of West Africa, for instance, an important festival takes place near the beginning of August to mark the beginning of the yam harvest. In Nigeria, the New Yam Festival is an annual cultural event lasting two days. The festival has its origins in the beliefs of the indigenous Ibo and Yoruba tribes. To the Ibo, the festival is called Iri Ji, *ji* meaning yam; the Yoruba call the festival Eje. Singing, dancing, drumming, and a parade are prominent aspects of the festivities, which carry spiritual overtones throughout. Thanks are given to deities and spirits of the earth and sky for the blessing of the yam harvest, and the yams are then harvested and blessed. A feast featuring the freshly gathered yams ensues.

In Ghana, the Ga people celebrate the Homowo Festival in August. *Homowo* translates as "hoot at hunger." A special ritual food is prepared and offerings are made to the ancestors. Dancing, drumming, and sharing of food are important aspects of the celebration (Mazama, 305).

In Russia also, August was a time to give thanks for agricultural blessings and to pray for greater abundance. Several celebrations were held throughout the month, each one dedicated to a "savior" who served the role of personified nature spirit. August 1 was celebrated as the day of the Honey Savior, or Wet Savior, and on this day, honey was gathered and water sources were blessed. August 6 marked the day of the Apple Savior. To eat an apple before this date was considered taboo, and the only atonement was to abstain from apples for a full forty days. Apples were first harvested on this day, and prayers were uttered over the newly picked fruits. August 16 was dedicated to the Nut Savior, as nuts were harvested at this time (Ivanits, 24).

August was a special time for the ancient Romans, as well. August 1 was celebrated with a feast in honor of Augustus Caesar who founded the Roman Empire, and ceremonies in honor of the dedication of the temples of Victoria Virgo, goddess of victory, were also held (Futrell, 81). August 21 was celebrated with the Consualia festival held in honor of Consus, a god associated with harvested fruit and grain. The Consualia included horse racing as well as an underground altar that was unearthed and raised up as part of the ceremony. Offerings of burnt first fruits were made to Consus in thanksgiving for a successful harvest (Takács, 55–56). August 25 was dedicated to the goddess Ops. Also known as Opis, she was a goddess of abundance and plenty. Called the Opiconsivia, her festival celebrated the successful storing of the harvest (Takács, 55–56).

As Rome became Christianized, so too did its Pagan celebrations. August 1, for example, which had been previously dedicated to the non-Christian Augustus Caesar and to the Pagan goddess of victory, became instead a day to honor Saint Peter, one of the twelve apostles of Jesus. Jesus is one of the central figures of Christian theology, seen as a messiah, or savior/liberator. According to legend, Saint Peter was imprisoned by King Herod of Judea for his Christian beliefs and alignment with Jesus. Though chained at his arms and legs and heavily guarded, Peter miraculously escaped, an angel having appeared to him to free him of his chains and open the gates leading out of the prison so that he could safely pass through. Legend holds that one of the chains that had bound Peter passed into the hands of Eudoxia, daughter of the Roman Emperor Theodosis II, while another of the chains was kept by the Pope. According to lore, when the Pope showed Eudoxia his part of Peter's chain, the two chains joined together to form one single chain, a miracle that led Eudoxia to proclaim the day of this occurrence (which happened to be at the start of August) as a day to honor Saint Peter and celebrate his liberation from bondage. This holiday came to be known as the Feast of Saint Peter ad Vincula, or the Feast of Saint Peter in chains. By creating a new Christian holiday on top of an existing Pagan one, August 1 was effectively appropriated as a church holiday (Pruen, 148). By the seventh century, the Feast of Saint Peter in Chains was a well-established tradition in Rome. Filings from the chains were supposed to have supernatural powers, and were kept by the Popes and given as gifts to bestow great favor and honor (Addis, 656–657). In the early English Church, the Feast of St. Peter in Chains was celebrated as a harvest festival. Loaves of bread were made from the first fruits of the corn harvest, which were then brought to the church to be consecrated (Rhys, 8).

The idea of the first fruits of a harvest being sacred is extremely widespread. Early liturgical books such as *De Ceremoniis*, a work attributed to the Emperor Constantine VII, who ruled the Byzantine Empire from 913 to 959, describe a custom that took place on either August 1 or 6. The Emperor and the Patriarch would lead a grand procession from the palace to a nearby vineyard, where the Patriarch would make a blessing over a basket of grapes from the harvest. The Emperor would then give a grape to each nobleman or officer in attendance. The ceremony was intended as a blessing for the new grapes that the harvest had provided (Gomme).

The Jewish culture held first fruits to be sacred, as well. At the beginning of the harvest, priests would go out into the fields and collect the first ripe corn. Then, accompanied by a large crowd, the new corn would be carried in procession back to the temple. The procession was sometimes led by an ox who had been adorned with an olive crown, and pipe music was played as the party approached the city. Upon arrival, the corn would be displayed with great pomp, then it was blessed and offered to their god Jehovah as an offering (Hartwell, 323).

The apostle Saint Paul makes interesting mention of the first-fruits tradition, relating the well-known and common first-fruits sacrifice to the body, life, and symbolism of the Christian messiah Jesus. The first book of Corinthians in the King James Bible, chapter 15, verse 20, says, "But now is Christ risen from the dead, and become the first-fruits of them that slept"(Ibid.). By relating the idea of the christ to the idea of the first-fruits, a connection was forged between older Pagan symbols and newer symbols introduced by Christianity. We find yet more Pagan harvest symbolism in the Christian concept of communion. Based on the biblical tale of Jesus offering bread to his followers along with the words "Take, eat; this is my body," communion is a religious ritual in which Christians eat blessed bread (sometimes referred to as the Eucharist) as a way to commune with and connect to the spirit of Jesus (Matthew 26:26). Just as Pagans might view the harvested crops as the outer manifestation of the "body" of nature's Great Work, Christians might view the Eucharist as a symbol of the body of Jesus, himself an embodiment of sacrifice for the sake of life. In Communion, Christians might eat a small piece of consecrated bread, viewing it either as a symbol of or as the actual body of Christ, just as Pagans at Lughnasadh might view the first fruits of the harvest and the bread made from it as a symbolic or actual embodiment of nature's incredible gift. As Pagans find grace, love, comfort, hope, and beauty in the harvest and the fact that nature gives us her best, perpetuating the growth cycle of the plants of Earth so that her creatures might eat and live, many Christians find the same virtues in the story of their Jesus's acceptance of death so that humankind might have a chance to endure. Despite the variance in symbols and differences in cultural practices, we find common themes of sacrifice, gratitude, hope, and renewal throughout our many harvest-themed spiritual rites around the world. This Lughnasadh, why not combine the practices of many cultures to create your own personally significant and satisfying harvest celebration? In the next chapter, we'll survey many ways in which modern Pagans far and wide celebrate this blessed day.

NEW WAYS

tion, introspection, discernment, sacrifice, excellent time for mag-

ity, abundance, strength, growth, protection, honoring ancestors,

nsformation, or communications with the dead, sacred wells, he

ls for magick, astronomical midpoint between the Summer, So

n at 15 degrees Leo in the Northern Hemisphere, Sun a

quarius in the Southern Hemisphere, Mother Goddess, Ear

Goddess, water nymphs, tree nymphs, the spirit of the land,

, Earth God, Solar God, the warrior, the protector, the sa

the dying god, the spirit of vegetation, the newly crowned king

, Dryads, Demeter, Kore, Inannotar, Nemesis, Ops, U

, Juturna, Stata Mater, Danu, Artemis, Osiris, L

tenhile, Consus, Thor, Vulcan, Thoth, Lahi, Vertumnus,

lar energies, happiness, transformation. Brown: Earth energies,

Illumination, success, divine power, harvest Green: Abundan

, vegetation Herb Blackberry: Protection, binding, defense, h

healing, abundance, friendship, love Allspice: Money, weal

magickal power Basil: Protection, luck, love, wealth, abundan

Solar energies, healing, protection, friendship, peace, prospe

$\mathcal{F}$OR MANY PAGANS who want to celebrate the early August sabbat, it's often challenging to find the *uniqueness* of this holiday. Lughnasadh is one of *three* harvest celebrations, and as few of us do more than keep a small garden, it's easy to understand the difficulty many of us encounter in making our August sabbat rites personally significant and meaningful in our own modern-day lives. While Samhain marks the third harvest and end of the growing season, and the Fall Equinox (a.k.a. Mabon) marks the second harvest and the middle of the harvest season, Lughnasadh happens at the very start of the harvest season, marking the point where the first fruit of the land has at last reached maturity. There is more harvest to come, but right now the joy is in knowing that the harvest *will* come.

Like the promise of a rainbow, our first harvest of the season reassures us that if all continues to go well, we can expect more wholesome treasures down the road that will sustain us throughout the winter. But what does this mean in your own life? It's not like you can't just run down to the store and pick up some fruits and vegetables whenever you need them, so what's the point in celebrating a harvest your own life doesn't utterly depend upon? You probably already spot the fallacy in that line of thinking: our lives *do* depend on that harvest, every bit as much as our agriculturally minded ancestors depended on it. We know the foodstuffs don't just magickally appear at the market, of course, but if we're not personally tilling the land, planting the seeds, and tending to the crops day in and day out until harvest time, it's very easy to push that fact to the back of our minds. Considering what would happen to us if the harvest *did* fail and the food *didn't* make it to the market can serve as a solid reminder of how much we really do depend on the earth to sustain us. Our modern lives are designed to make us feel as independent from our natural environment as possible but it's only an illusion.

The earth is our mother; even if we're wearing three-piece suits, driving fancy cars, and basking in carpeted, air-conditioned luxury, we're needy children, totally dependent on the earth to provide us with food, water, shelter, and clothing. Where would you be if an asteroid crashed into our planet? What would happen to you if every plant on the earth withered and died? It would be horrible, right? Luckily, that hasn't happened—and this luck is the joy of Lughnasadh. It's the gratitude we feel for life, the thankfulness we express for our continued existence. It's the delight of seeing the first signs of effort beginning to pay off. It's the beginning of the culmination of summertime's toil and what the earth has sowed. What you personally have sowed is also now in the early stages of being reaped. In this chapter, you'll discover many ways in which modern Pagans celebrate Lughnasadh. Let these ideas inspire you to create your own personally meaningful sabbat rites!

Modern Themes and Common Elements

While there is certainly no set standard of modern Pagan Lughnasadh customs, there are definitely some widespread commonalities worth noting. Themes of harvest, gratitude, and reflection are abundant, as the holiday is commonly seen as a time to celebrate the ending of summer while looking forward to the coming fall. Potlucks, picnics, and other forms of feasting are popular, and the gathering of wild herbs is also widely practiced. Magick and rituals frequently focus on abundance, protection, and fertility, though themes of death and shedding away the old are also common. Offerings are usually given, though recipients vary widely, from specific deities like Danu or Lugh, to ancestors or to the dead in general. Still others make offerings at Lughnasadh to nature spirits like dryads and other types of vegetation-protecting nymphs. Despite the differences in our personal practices, our Lughnasadh offerings share a universal and simple message: "Thanks!"

Lughnasadh in the Country

For Pagans living in rural areas, Lughnasadh celebrations are likely to center around agriculture. Many rural Pagans have their own gardens or crops to tend, and their own first harvests to pull in, come Lughnasadh. There's something magickal about growing a plant from seed to full maturity: you see the culmination of effort and energy expended by yourself, the sun, the earth, the elements, and the plant itself; you witness first-hand the great mystery of sacrifice for the sake of life. Rural gardening Pagans have a definite advantage here in connecting to the ebb and flow of the Lughnasadh season.

Popular Lughnasadh activities for rural Pagans include harvesting crops, picking wild herbs or berries, and enjoying an evening bonfire. Cooking and feasting are also primary aspects of Lughnasadh celebration for many rural Pagans, with foods highlighting the best of the harvest. It's a traditional time to prepare berry jams and preserves, make fruit pies or nut pies, roast potatoes or other root vegetables, and bake up a fresh loaf of bread. Magick and ritual are often carried out fireside, waterside, or on hilltops, and offerings of "first fruits" from the harvest or foods prepared from these plants may be presented as an expression of gratitude for the sacrifice required in manifesting the current bounty. August is also a popular time for country fairs, giving some rural Pagans yet another way to celebrate the season.

Lughnasadh in the City

Pagans in urban areas find both challenges and benefits in city living when it comes to Lughnasadh celebrations. Sure, there might not be a place to build a bonfire or a swatch of woods in which to search for wild berries, but on the bright side there are a lot more people around with whom to celebrate. Big cities often have established and open Pagan communities, so many urban Pagans attend sabbat gatherings with other local celebrants. These celebrations can range in size from a few buddies to a large festival crowd of hundreds. Activities such as feasting, drumming, dancing, and ritual are often the highlights. Many city Pagans enjoy feasting with family, friends, and neighbors, with fruits, vegetables, and bread featured prominently as culinary fare. The food may be seen as sacred and magickal, symbolizing nature's glory and a gift from the earth, even if it more recently came from the grocery store.

There's just no substituting for the great outdoors, however; many city Pagans find Lughnasadh to be the perfect time to seek it out, even if it requires a drive, bus ride, or a little creativity. A bike ride in the park, a drive to the country, or simply noticing the beauty of parking lot trees, office building shrubbery, and other city foliage can be very refreshing Lughnasadh activities for urban dwellers.

Different Pagans, Different Practices

Following is a sampling of several Pagan "denominations," and a brief look at some ways those particular denominations might choose to celebrate the Lughnasadh sabbat. Keep in mind, however, that Pagans are a diverse bunch, and even amongst the practitioners of the same particular Pagan path or tradition, there is still great difference in practice and belief from group to group, place to place, and person to person.

Celtic Reconstructionist

Celtic Reconstructionists base their beliefs and practices on the historically verified rites and rituals of the ancient Celts, aiming to recreate the old religion as closely as possible. Many Celtic Reconstructionists hold a celebration of *Lá Lúnasa*, or *Tailtiu*, at the beginning or middle of August. The festival is often timed to coincide with the local berry season, with locally grown, in-season berries the star of the show. Wild berry picking is a popular *Lá Lúnasa* activity enjoyed by Celtic Reconstructionists young and old. Feasts with family, friends, and neighbors are popular forms of celebration, with berries being featured in every dish on the menu from main course to dessert. Berry sauces, berry pies, berry jams, berry vinegar, berry muffins, and other berry-infused dishes may be served. Celtic Reconstructionists in the northeastern United States commonly celebrate with the regionally grown blueberries, while

Celtic Reconstructionists in the Pacific Northwest tend to celebrate with local blackberries.

Many *Lá Lúnasa* celebrations include a ceremonial offering. Berries or other foods are often presented to the gods and to the spirits of the land. Some Celtic Reconstructionists living in hurricane-prone areas present offerings to the god Lugh or to the Cailleachan, a class of storm hags. First fruits from the harvest might be given, poems might be recited, and favorite libations might be offered in hopes of gaining protection from weather-related dangers and disasters.

Wiccan

Wicca is a modern, earth-honoring religion founded in a belief in both a male and a female deity, magick, and reincarnation. Wiccan spirituality varies widely, but a majority of Wiccans do honor the eight sabbats of the Wheel of the Year, including Lughnasadh. The start of August might be celebrated as Lughnasadh, Lammas, or August Eve. Rituals and feasts are common, and the holiday is often seen as a time to give thanks for blessings and to celebrate our own skills and efforts. Prayers may be uttered and offerings may be given to the god of grain and to the goddess earth, with bread and fruit being popular gifts for the deities. Other activities might include games, baking, arts and crafts, crop harvesting, and simple get-togethers with family and friends.

Heathen / Asatru

Heathenry encompasses Asatru and other Neopagan paths which practice the pre-Christian religious traditions of Germany, Scandinavia, and other places in northern Europe. Adherents of the Asatru path celebrate July 29 as Stikklestad Day, commemorating the day that Olaf the Lawbreaker was killed in battle. Olaf was responsible for the oppression, maiming, and death of many Norwegians who refused to convert to Christianity, so many followers of Asatru use Stikklestad Day as a time to honor the bravery of the martyrs and warriors who fought and died rather than submit to Olaf's cause.

On August 9, many Asatru Heathens celebrate a Day of Rememberance for Radbod. Radbod was a king of Frisia who drew the attention of Christian missionaries who aimed to convert him. Radbod was insulted by the assertion of the missionaries that his Asatru ancestors were likely burning in hell, and he boldly refused conversion and expelled the missionaries. Many Asatru Heathens remember Radbod on this day by drinking a toast out of a horn in his honor.

August 19 is a celebration called Freyfaxi, originally marking the time of harvest in ancient Iceland. Freyfaxi can also be celebrated on August 1 or August 23. The powers of fertility are honored at Freyfaxi, and many modern Asatru Heathens celebrate the day with a blot (a special Asatru ritual involving feast and sacrifice) to Frey, brother of Freya and ruler of rain, sunshine, and growing produce. There is often a large feast in celebration of the harvest (Craigie, 27).

(Modern) Druid

Modern Druids are often of an eclectic style, picking and choosing from ancient Celtic beliefs and adapting these for current times, meshing new innovations with various time-honored traditions to create a personally relevant practice. Modern Druids might celebrate Lughnasadh on August 1st, on the midway point between the summer solstice and fall equinox, or on the night of full moon in August.

Lughnasadh is often celebrated by modern Druids as the wedding feast of the Celtic god Lugh, an occasion held to honor Lugh's symbolic marriage to the land. As the wielder of the unstoppable Spear of Victory, Lugh, a god of lightning (among other things), is thought capable of protecting the crops from the potential destruction of storms and other threats. The symbol of Lugh's spear is frequently woven into Lughnasadh rites and rituals.

Traditionally, Lughnasadh was a time when many tribes would gather together, and many modern Druids continue this tradition by celebrating the day with other groves, working groups much like the Wiccan coven. For modern Druids, Lughnasadh is also a time for celebration of the first harvest, as many crops are now beginning to ripen. Offerings are often given in hopes of gaining protection for the crops and ensuring a bountiful harvest to come, with blessed bread and beer among the most favored gifts for the gods. Wild-harvested foods are also sometimes incorporated into ritual, and drumming is often used to help raise and maintain energy throughout the ceremony. Like the ancients, many modern Druids find Lughnasadh to be an ideal time for making pacts and sealing oaths, and it's fairly common for handfastings to be performed and contracts to be signed on this occasion.

Traditional Witchcraft

Traditional Witchcraft is a religion whose practices are based in pre-Christian animism, traditional folk magick, and an often polytheistic belief system. Traditional Witchcraft is different from the modern religion of Wicca in that its rituals and beliefs are founded in local and regional cultural traditions, whereas Wicca welcomes contemporary invention and embraces an eclectic combination of various religious or shamanic systems. Specific practices in Traditional Witchcraft differ from place to place, based on local traditions, personal heritage, and the regional environment in which the practitioner dwells. Some Traditional Witches celebrate each of the four cross-quarter days such as Lughnasadh, and some celebrate the equinoxes and solstices, but most do not celebrate both. Traditional Witches may celebrate the day as the Celtic Lughnasadh, or as the Anglo-

Saxon Lammas. Practices generally stick to traditional customs such as singing, dancing, making offerings, and enjoying a feast. Brooms might be ridden through the fields as a way to banish any energies of decay and to welcome in a spirit of increase and growth, just as certain witches of Buckinghamshire did three generations ago.

Neopagan

Neopaganism is a term defining a broad and varied category of practitioners engaged in any number of forms of nature-based spirituality or new takes on old Pagan religions and practices. Neopagans include Wiccans, eclectic witches, modern Druids, and others—nearly anyone living in modern times who defines themselves as a Pagan is also a Neopagan by definition, as it essentially means "new Pagan." Neopagans are modern practioners of non-Abrahamic, non-monotheistic spiritual or magickal practice which is often understood within a contemporary context that can be adapted for modern times.

Neopagans may celebrate Lughnasadh or Lammas individually or with a group. Many Neopagan groups host community rituals for each of the sabbats, including Lughnasadh. Although Lughnasadh and Lammas are two distinct holidays, Neopagan celebrations frequently combine elements of both traditions. Giving thanks for the harvest and mourning for the symbolic death of the corn king or other personified vegetation spirit is often the focus of such celebrations, and feasting is a popular activity. Potlucks and picnics might be hosted in private homes, local parks, or on the tops of hills. Many Neopagans view the Lughanasadh sabbat as a time of reflection, a time of thanksgiving and gratitude, and a time to celebrate the cycles of life. Magick for protection, prosperity, and abundance is commonly performed, and rituals often focus on themes of gratitude and sacrifice. Offerings of food or libations may be shared with the spirits. Corn dollies and other harvest-themed crafts may be incorporated, and drumming, singing, chanting, dancing, and general merrymaking are frequently part of the celebration.

Eclectic Witchcraft

Eclectic Witchcraft is a term defining practitioners of Witchcraft who may or may not choose to define themselves as Wiccan. Eclectic witches create their own personalized belief systems and magickal methods by drawing on practices and beliefs from a variety of traditions, cultures, and spiritual systems. Nature's energies and cycles are often of central importance to eclectic witches, and seasonal tide shifts are usually marked with celebration, magick, and ritual. There is no set way in which eclectic witches celebrate Lughnasadh. Rituals may be focused on themes of abundance, harvest, sacrifice, thanksgiving, seasonal changes, or other themes the individual eclectic witch deems appropriate. An eclectic witch might choose to celebrate the holiday with a feast and ritual in honor of the harvest and the spirits of abundance, and the sacrifice made by the spirit of the harvested crops may be acknowledged at this time. Games, sports, outdoor gatherings, and picnics offer additional options for sabbat entertainment, and berry picking and wild herb gathering are also frequently practiced.

Modern Gatherings and Festivals

Here's a sampling of some August festivals worth visiting. Some of these are modern Pagan gatherings focused on the magickal significance and celebration of the Lughnasadh or Lammas sabbat. Others are not especially related to Lughnasadh or Lammas, but as celebrations of the first harvest or examples of the traditional late summer country fair, these activities are very much in line with our August celebrations.

Green Spirit Festival

Sponsored by Circle Sanctuary, a nonprofit international Nature Spirituality resource center and legally recognized Shamanic Wiccan church, the Green Spirit Festival has been held annually since 2005 at the 200-acre Circle Sanctuary Nature Preserve near Barneveld, Wisconsin. Featuring rituals, workshops, drumming, dancing, feasting, nature walks, a mugwort harvest, a stone circle, and much more, this three-day, family-friendly camping event brings together Pagans from all over the country. For more information about the Green Spirit Festival, see the Circle Sanctuary website at www.circlesanctuary .org/index.php/our-events/festivals/green-spirit.

Iowa Lammasfest

Held annually at the beginning of August at the beautiful Cottonwood Campground in the Coralville Dam area of Iowa, the Iowa Lammasfest brings Pagans together for a three-day family-friendly camp-out and harvest celebration. Founded in 2003, festival highlights include a harvest feast, a Lammas ritual, a children's area, and a variety of Pagan-themed workshops. Proceeds from the Iowa Lammasfest benefit the Macbride Raptor Project, an Iowa-based organization dedicated to preserving the state's birds of prey and their natural habitats. For more information about Iowa Lammasfest, see their website at http:// www.lammasfest.us/home.php.

Sacred Harvest Festival

The Sacred Harvest Festival is a nine-day celebration of community and magick held each year in early August in a grove of century-old oaks near St. Paul, Minnesota. Founded in 1998 by Harmony Tribe, a nonprofit organization providing spiritual experiences and educational opportunities for practitioners of nature-based spirituality, the Sacred Harvest Festival draws together crowds of hundreds and often attracts nationally recognized spiritual leaders and guest speakers from around the country. Spanning the course of two full weekends and all the days in between, the festival creates a sense of tribal Pagan community as the blessings of the harvest are celebrated. Highlights include a Sacred Spirit Hunt ritual, Rites of Passage rituals and other special rituals, drumming, dancing, workshops, a central sacred fire, and more. The festival is family-friendly, and boasts a large percentage of children and teens in attendance each year. For more information, visit http:// harmonytribe.org/content/sacred-harvest-festival.

Santo Domingo Pueblo Feast Day and Green Corn Dance

Every year on August 4 at the Santo Domingo Pueblo about 40 miles north of Albuquerque, New Mexico, Pueblo tribes from the region gather together to host an annual feast day and Green Corn Dance. More than a thousand members of Pueblo tribes participate each year, and the ceremonies are open to outside visitors who flock to Santo Domingo in crowds of several thousand to witness the sacred spectacle. The feast day of Saint Dominic, the patron saint of the Santo Domingo Pueblo, the holiday is an interesting blending of ancient tribal custom and the influence of modern Catholicism. A morning mass starts the day, after which a statue of Saint Dominic is carried from the church to a central place in the plaza where it is placed in a shrine. The shrine is decorated with greenery, and candles and traditional rugs are placed to the sides of the statue. Later, the sound of drums and chanting fills the air as men, women, and children dance in the plaza in honor of the green corn and in gratitude for the beginning of the harvest. Potters, jewelry-makers, and other artisans display their wares for the shopping pleasure of spectators, and there is even an area with carnival rides. Photography and video recording is not permitted at the ceremony, but visitors from around the world are welcome to attend. For more information, see the Santo Domingo Pueblo website at http://www .santodomingotribe.com/feastday-3/.

Tullamore Show

Want to celebrate Lughnasadh with a traditional country fair? If big and authentic is what you're looking for, you'd be hard pressed to beat Ireland's annual Tullamore Show. The Tullamore Show held annually towards the beginning of August is Ireland's largest single-day festival and premier agricultural gathering of the year. Held annually towards the beginning of August on a beautiful 250-acre portion of the Butterfield Estate in Tullamore, County Offaly, Ireland, the festival boasts crowds of 60,000-plus, drawing local, national, and international visitors. Permanently revived in its modern form in 1991, the very first agricultural fair held in Tullamore took place in 1840. Featuring livestock exhibitions and competitions, horticulture competitions, sheepdog trials and other dog events, home industries, new inventions, farming and cooking skill demonstrations, food, arts, crafts, vintage farming equipment, fashion, performing arts, and even an occasional team of dancing horses, the Tullamore Show offers an authentic cultural experience of the traditional Irish country fair along with many additional, more contemporary attractions. For more information, visit the Tullamore Show website at http://tullamoreshow.com/.

Lughnasa Festival at Craggaunowen

Held annually in early August in County Clare, Ireland, the Craggaunowen Lughnasa Festival features displays and demonstrations of Ireland's history and rich cultural heritage. Festival-goers witness costumed reenactments of hand-to-hand combat, view weapons, examine artifacts, enjoy period fashions and jewelry, learn about historic crafts and cooking techniques, and explore other aspects of everyday life in Ireland spanning from the Bronze age through the sixteenth century. For more information, see their website at http://www.shannonheritage.com/Events/AnnualEvents/LughnasaFestival/.

Timoleague Festival

The Timoleague Festival is a ten-day harvest celebration held annually in August in Timoleague, West Cork, Ireland. The festival features foot races, pig racing, music, fancy dress competitions, comedy acts, and other entertainment. For more information, see the Timoleague Festival page at http://www .timoleague.ie/timoleague_festival.html.

Eastbourne Lammas Festival

Held annually since 2001, the Eastbourne Lammas Festival is a free, family-friendly festival of music, dance, and entertainment held at a seaside park each year in Eastbourne, East Sussex, England, right around Lammas time. The festival includes a seafront, costumed procession led by two masked giants representing Herne and Andred, two local characters whose oversized costumes are fashioned from wicker and papier mâché. There's also a Lammas ritual honoring John Barleycorn (a personification of the barley crop from which alcoholic beverages are made) plus a wide variety of Morris dancers, an open-air *ceilidh* (a traditional Gaelic social gathering often featuring folk music, dance, and storytelling as the primary means of entertainment), arts, crafts, drumming, storytelling, skill and craft demonstrations, vendors, food, beer, picnicking, and more. The volunteer-run festival raises money for the Royal National Lifeboat Institution, a charity organization founded in 1824 providing twenty-four-hour on-call lifeboat search and rescue around Ireland and the U.K. For more information about the Eastbourne Lammas Festival, see the festival website at http://www.lammasfest.org/.

St. Andrew's Lammas Fair

Its origins in medieval times, the St. Andrew's Lammas Fair holds the title of Europe's oldest surviving street fair. Held annually for five days in early August in St. Andrew's, Scotland, the fair fills two of the towns widest streets with vendor stalls, carnival rides, concerts, and other attractions. Originally held as a religious observance and employment fair, the Lammas Fair has evolved into a purely secular event drawing together crowds of thousands from all over the region.

Suggested Activities

There are many avenues of adventure and exploration open to you in regards to celebrating the August sabbat. The energy flow of this season has a very interesting and rather unusual quality about it that has special purpose and benefits in the magickal arts. Summer is ending but autumn has not yet begun; the sun is past its apex but has yet to reach its nadir, or low point. The immediate worry of hunger is subsiding as the crops ripen but the anxiety of successfully bringing in the rest of the harvest lingers. Summer leisure is coming to a close just as the extra toil of the harvest season begins. We're starting to see the results of our summertime efforts but the reaping is not yet complete.

The August sabbat is both an opening and a closing, a culmination and a commencement. It's the in-between time just after the heat of the day and right before sunset; it's the crossroads where seemingly contrasting and contradictory forces join together to form an open path extending in all directions. Magickally, it's a great time for highly transformative workings, as the energy flow can be used as a sort of doorway or portal into dimensions you might not be able to easily access regularly. The Lughnasadh sabbat provides an opportunity to go down the rabbit hole, through the key hole, or through the looking glass; you'll be able to work more extreme magick on a grander scale if you take advantage of the in-between, undefined, and therefore *limitless* nature of the season.

Try working magick you ordinarily wouldn't; challenge your limitations and suspend doubt long enough to give it a shot. Think you don't have a chance of landing your dream job or getting some other super-rare and fabulous opportunity? Think you're not powerful enough to change the world in any significant way? Give yourself some extra luck with a bit of Lughnasadh magick and you might just be surprised at what all you can do!

Lughnasadh is also a great season for reflection, introspection, and reconnection—with the earth, ourselves, and the other inhabitants of our precious planet. Spend some time in nature thinking and reflecting, contemplating and dreaming. Observe the plants and animals around you, and notice how the seasons are nearing a shift as you ponder the shifts and changes in your own life. Reconnect with friends and family by hosting or attending a get-together, and reconnect with the rest of humanity through volunteer service work or just getting out and about among the people for a little fun and socializing. You might also consider reconnecting to your loved ones who have passed on by engaging in rituals, meditations, or other activities intended to honor the dead or communicate with them.

Since it's harvest time, feasting, berry-picking, herb gathering, and similar activities are also effective ways to tune in to Lughnasadh's energy flow. Consider visiting a local farm or farmer's market or taking a drive out to the woods or countryside to get back in touch with the spirit of the living earth.

Your Lughnasadh celebration might focus on harvest, honoring the dead, reflection, sacrifice, human craft and skill, or a number of other possibilities. Here are some specific ideas for activities to try this time of year to help you make the most of this blessed season.

Honor the Dead

As the time of year when the Tailitu fair was held in honor of Lugh's fallen mother, Lughnasadh is an opportunity to follow tradition by honoring the dead. Death is something we all come to face. We lose loved ones, we see death happening every day, and we know that we too will have to face the Reaper sooner or later. At this time of year, the first ripened fruits of the harvest lose their life to the scythe so that we may continue to live. Every creature experience death, and Nature itself experiences death as well. Life and death are connected, both integral parts of the cycle of existence. Why not spend some time this Lughnasadh contemplating death and honoring those who have passed away and moved on from life's corporeal form?

You might visit a local cemetery, perhaps bringing along a picnic lunch to enjoy graveside, or leaving an offering of flowers, fruit, or libations for those who are buried. If you have a very old or neglected cemetery nearby, you might do a bit of grave maintenance: remove weeds, pick up trash, and put back in place any fallen gravestones.

You might also decide to engage in some genealogical research, honoring your dead ancestors by finding out who they were, where they lived, and what they did. Search for old photos of deceased loved ones, and place these prominently in your home or on your altar as a reminder of the necessity of death and as a tribute to the lives of those who have passed on.

Bring in the Harvest

Just because you might not have a farm or garden of your own doesn't mean you can't get in on the action of the first harvest season! Many farms open their gates this time of year to anyone who wants to come pick their own fruits and vegetables and experience both the pleasure and toil of the harvest firsthand. You might find a pick-your-own-berries or pick-your-own-beans operation a lot closer to your town than you think. If there aren't any farms in your area, go wild. Explore the woods or other natural areas where you live and look for plants you can use for magick, food, and other purposes. Wild onion, mint, and dandelion leaves are all edible and magickally useful. You might even find some wild blackberries growing in your area. Just be sure not to eat or drink anything you find outside unless you're absolutely positive what it is and absolutely positive that it's not poisonous. Many totally safe plants have very toxic lookalikes, so be careful. If you're not sure about an ingredient, use it instead for an herbal sachet, toss it in a batch of potpourri, or reserve it for another magickal purpose that doesn't involve consuming the questionable herb.

When harvesting plants outdoors, please don't take plants from areas that are especially environmentally vulnerable (like protected areas or rapidly eroding banks, for instance), and never take more than one-fourth of a plant's total mass, at most.

Go Magickal Tool Hunting

With pleasant temperatures, beautiful foliage, and not a snowflake in sight, Lughnasadh is an excellent time to scout out some new magick tools in the great outdoors. In many places, the ground will soon be covered with fallen leaves, and later, with snow, so why not take advantage of the visible, virtually uncovered ground and look for some treasures there? You might find a fallen branch to use for a magickal staff, or a fallen stick you might use for a witch's wand. Clean the stick or branch, remove sharp pieces, and, if you wish, decorate your new magickal tool with painted or engraved symbols, words, or other designs. Resist the urge to harvest sticks and branches from living trees—you can find plenty on the ground that are already fallen and ready for use. Also look for stones you find appealing. You might use the stones for spellwork, as part of a magickal charm bag, a meditation aid, or an addition to a wand or other tool. You might even craft your own set of runes out of the stones you find. Just be aware that some natural areas have a "take nothing" policy, interpreted very strictly where "nothing" includes a tiny pebble, the smallest twig, or even an infinitesimal scrap of tree bark. There are reasons for a restriction like this, so if you encounter it please obey the rules. Wherever you live, there are places to go where you can legally (and without risking environmental damage) harvest a few sticks or stones without issue.

Get Cookin'

Feasting is a traditional part of harvest celebrations around the world, so why not be a part of this longstanding magickal continuum and do a bit of cooking (and feasting) yourself? Some people are intimidated by cooking, just like others might be intimidated by a complex mathematical equation. The great thing about cooking, though, is that it doesn't have to be complicated. Cooking with fresh, unprocessed ingredients is actually much more simple than cooking from boxes and cans, not to mention more delicious and spiritually fulfilling. Working with raw ingredients brings us closer to the earth because the foods we are using are much closer to it as well. Rather than opening up a box of something-or-other packed full of chemical preservatives and synthetic flavorings far removed from the farm where it originally grew, opt instead for fresh ingredients you can easily imagine growing right out of the ground. A freshly harvested sampling of seasonal veggies doesn't need many extras to make it delicious; just a pinch of salt, pepper, rosemary, garlic, or another herb or spice, and the food's natural flavor does the rest. If you want to get fancy, try making a loaf of bread from scratch. Baking bread is an activity that's accessible to almost anyone—

not nearly as hard as it might seem. Many bread recipes don't require the use of yeast or other tricky-to-use rising agents. For example, traditional Irish soda bread is virtually foolproof and has only three basic ingredients: flour, buttermilk, and baking soda. And if you do want to use yeast to make a dough that rises, the trick is to make sure your water temperature is in the right range. Using a thermometer takes the guesswork out of it and helps ensure success. If you really have no desire to flex your culinary muscles, you can still enjoy a fantastic feast. Get your friends and family involved by inviting everyone to come over for a big potluck dinner. You'll be able to get away with preparing or purchasing just one or two dishes and your guests can bring the rest! Outdoor dining is especially popular this time of year, so consider taking your Lughnasadh feast outdoors at sunset to watch the fading sunlight as you eat and reminisce about the good times of summer.

Play Games

Lughnasadh was traditionally a time for competitive sports and games, a time to show off human skill and athletic prowess. If you're a sporty sort, you might want to host your own miniature Tailteann Fair, inviting your friends over for a game of football, frisbee, a foot race, or other competitive displays of skill. Choose a sport or activity everyone will enjoy, and keep the games lighthearted and good-humored. You might throw in a sack race or two to up the silly quotient and ensure your gamers have a good time. Give prizes to the winners: ribbons, a crazy hat, or a decorated broom all make excellent trophies.

SPELLS
AND
DIVINATION

...ion, introspection, discernment, sacrifice, excellent time for image...

...ty, abundance, strength, growth, protection, honoring ancestors,

...sformation, or communications with the dead, sacred wells, he...

...s for magick, astronomical midpoint between the Summer So...

...at 15 degrees Leo in the Northern Hemisphere, Sun at...

...uarius in the Southern Hemisphere, Mother Goddess, Earth...

Goddess, water nymphs, tree nymphs, the spirit of the land,

Earth God, Solar God, the warrior, the protector, the sac...

...he dying god, the spirit of vegetation, the newly crowned king,

...Dryads, Demeter, Kore, Luonnotar, Nemesis, Ops, Na...

...Juturna, Stata Mater, Danu, Artemis, Osiris, Lug...

...achilli, Consus, Thor, Vulcan, Thoth, Loki, Vertumnus, ...

...er energies, happiness, transformation. Brown: Earth energies,

...llumination, success, divine power, harvest. Green: Abundance

...vegetation Herb Blackberry: Protection, binding, defense, ...

...healing, abundance, friendship, love. Allspice: Money, wealth,

...magickal power. Basil: Protection, luck, love, wealth, abundance

...Solar energies, healing, protection, friendship, peace, prosperi...

*L*UGHNASADH IS A time of both waning and waxing energies, a time of culmination and commencement marking the end of one era and the beginning of a new one as crops come to ripen and the real work of the harvest begins. This sabbat has a powerful, reflective, protective energy flow, making it an ideal time for spellwork and divination focused on safeguarding success, exploring gratitude, attracting prosperity, and welcoming good fortune. It's also a good time to gauge future prospects and evaluate past experiences through the art of divination. Here are a few spells and divination methods to try this Lughnasadh. These techniques can be adapted to fit your personal style and magickal needs; just open your mind, open your heart, and believe in your own abilities as a thinking, feeling human being.

Lughnasadh Spells

The heart of magick lies in the witch and not in the method, so as you work these spells, keep in mind that your emotional and mental state are key ingredients in the activation of each formula. Here you'll find instructions primarily outlining the outward form of each rite as well as hints about the inner alchemy that takes place in the mind and heart of the spellcaster. The magickal process is experienced slightly differently by each individual witch, so take these instructions as examples to help guide you in developing your own unique spellcasting techniques. These spells can be used anytime, but they're especially effective if worked on or near Lughnasadh.

Calm Down Candle Spell

In Greco-Roman culture, August was a month when feelings of anger, aggression, and desire were believed to be amplified by the intense heat and unrelenting brightness of the "dog days" of summer, named so after Sirius (the dog star), which became visible in the heavens at that time. The Greeks and Romans knew the stars as points of influence and beacons of guidance, and Sirius was thought to have a very strong, powerful, and aggressive energy flow capable of turning civilized humans nearly into salivating dogs, thirsty for relief and hungry for satisfaction. If you find yourself feeling uncomfortably agitated, upset, aggressive, on edge, or filled with such angst or desire that you can no longer think straight this August, try this simple candle spell to help you calm down fast.

You'll need an orange tealight candle (orange is symbolic of agitation and hunger) and a glass of water to work this spell. It can be cast indoors or outdoors, though if you're working the spell indoors, you'll need to find a space on the floor or near a window to serve as the magick space. Since this spell is designed to bring quick relief when you're feeling stressed, don't worry about doing any of the usual magickal preliminaries such as clearing your head, clearing the space, or casting a circle. When you're stressed, you won't be able to do any of those actions properly, so don't waste energy trying. Instead, get right to the heart of the magick.

Place the glass of water beside the candle. If you're working the spell outdoors, put the glass directly on the bare ground. If working the spell indoors, place the glass either on the floor or near a window—the idea is that you want the water to be in as close contact with the earth and its powerful energies as possible.

Take a deep breath and place your fingertips over the top of the candle. Let any feeling of anger, angst, irritation, stress, desires unfulfilled, etc. flow through you freely. Don't fight it; let your body be a funnel for these negative feelings, and honor these emotions while at the same time releasing your grip on them. It's okay to have negative feelings sometimes; such feelings serve to prove that essentially we are conscious, emotional, vulnerable creatures capable of hurting ourselves again and again for the sake of love and life, and that is indeed a beautiful and precious thing. We tend to store up this negativity, though, holding it with us as if our body was the bottle and our mind was the cork, which in turn can weigh down the spirit considerably. Instead, envision yourself as a tube, open on both ends. The stress pours in, yes, but it also can pour out easily and go right back to wherever it came from. Imagine yourself now as this tube, and let those stressful, negative, angry feelings flow out through your fingertips and into the candle wax.

Release your emotional energy into the wax until you feel completely drained and empty. You should have a hollow, rather indifferent feeling now in your heart and mind. If your emotions are still running strong, you're not yet done with this stage of the spell. Don't fight those feelings, and don't stop releasing those energies into the candle wax until you absolutely cannot release any more. Once you've reached that point, light the candle and relax your hands in your lap with your fingers held loosely and your palms facing upward.

Gaze at the flame and watch the wax melt in its heat and light, transformed into fuel for the fire. Imagine the negative energies you've poured into the candle wax transforming as well, turned into pure power to feed a hungry sun. Visualize the sun in the sky glowing brightly directly above the candle flame, and imagine the energy of the wax flowing upwards through the flame, through the sky, and straight to the shining sun. Say:

> *"I feed the sun the passion of my hunger!*
> *I feed the sun the power of my fears!*
> *I feed the sun the monster bred of injustice!*
> *I feed the sun the power of my tears!"*

Envision the energy flowing into the sun, instantly obliterated by the light and heat of that shining heavenly body. Now place your hands around the glass of water. Invite the energies of the Earth to flow into it. You can do this by visualizing with emotion things you associate with nature and the Earth element, perhaps imagining the feeling you get when admiring the beauty and power of lush forests, rich soil, and ancient rocks. Envision those energies entering into the glass of water, infusing the liquid with a strong, earthy vibration. If you like, directly invite the Earth element into the water by saying:

> *"Element of Earth, I call on you now!*
> *Please enter this glass of water, right here and now!*
> *Earth, come into this water right here and now!*
> *There is no other course; come into it now!"*

Now slowly take thirteen sips of the water, taking a deep breath between each drink and enjoying the beauty of the glowing candle flame as you do so. Notice the feeling the magickally charged water gives you; feel it nurturing your body, quenching both your physical and spiritual thirst with its heightened power. When you're finished, drip some of the remaining water on the candle to extinguish the flame. Take a final deep breath, exhaling long and deeply before returning to your regularly scheduled day.

Herbal Spell for Safeguarding Succcess

Lughnasadh is a traditional time for protection magick. The Irish Celts would lead their horses and cattle through water as a means of purification and protection, just as at Beltane, the livestock was led between two fires to achieve the same ends. Most likely, you don't have a whole lot of livestock sitting around, but that doesn't mean you don't have other valuables you'd like to protect. To the Celts, horses and cattle meant livelihood, survival, and prosperity—what elements of your own life can be similarly understood? Do you have money, resources, or a home that means the world to you? Have you gained success over the summer, or made progress towards any important goals? These assets are your valuables, your modern-day livestock, if you will. If you want to safeguard your success and progress and protect your valuables, try this simple spell based on the traditional Irish Lughnasadh practice for protecting livestock.

For this spell, you'll need to select a sampling of fresh herbs. Make a list of the assets and valuables you wish to protect, then choose a corresponding herb for each one. For example, you might choose basil, pine, or oregano to represent material wealth, or you might include lavender or rose petals to represent gains made in matters of the heart. You might select cinnamon to represent success and courage, or dandelion blossoms to represent happiness and joy. You can consult an herbal attributes guide for further ideas, follow your own intuition, or incorporate some of the suggestions here included. Ideally, you want the herbs you select to be fresh and large enough to handle. For instance, choose a sprig of fresh rosemary over a single dried rosemary leaf and choose a cinnamon stick over a loose pile of powdered cinnamon. If you include a dried, powdery herb, simply wrap it up in a bindle, tying it up in a small circle of cloth colored to correspond with the asset or valuable the particular herb represents.

Once you've gathered the herbs you'll be using, place them on your altar, lined up side by side horizontally along the altar's front edge. Now fill a large bowl about three-quarters full with water, and place this at the center of your altar. You can use water from a river, stream, or ocean, a bottle of spring water from the grocery store, collected rain water, or as a last resort, ordinary tap water. Invite the element of Water to enter into the bowl, envisioning its purifying qualities and thinking about the strength of a raging river, a powerful ocean wave, a downpour of heavy rain.

Now pick up the first herb and think hard about what it represents. Does this herb represent your wealth, your home, or your business success? Whatever it represents, think about the herb as if it actually *is* that thing. Visualize the represented asset or valuable in as many vivid details as possible, and project this into the herb. Say:

> *This is not (name of whatever herb it is, i.e., basil),*
> *but it is my (name of whatever asset or valuable the herb*
> *represents, i.e., financial success) that I hold in my hand.*

Now slowly drag the herb through the bowl of water, envisioning the water cleansing away any obstacles or impurities while infusing the represented asset or valuable with a protective strength. Say:

> *By the power of water, by river and sea,*
> *what I have is protected!*
> *So mote it be!*

Place the herb to the far side of the bowl of water. Repeat the process for each herb until all the herbs have been dragged through the water.

Now take the pile of wet herbs and the bowl of water outside to a natural place where you can feel the power and beauty of the earth. You'll also want to bring along an apple. Place the pile of herbs on the ground, and on top of this place the apple, stem pointing upwards. Pour the water from the bowl in a circle surrounding the herbs and the apple, saving a final few drops to sprinkle over the top of the magickal plant matter. Express your thanks for the continued welfare of your assets and valuables, and leave the apple and herbs outside as an additional offering of gratitude and goodwill.

Potato Spell for Good Luck and Good Fortune

As a traditional Lughnasadh staple, potatoes are a great medium for your sabbat magick. Try this simple spell to help attract good luck and increase good fortune. This spell involves a good amount of precision cutting, so be cautious and wear protective gloves while you work. To start, cut a potato in half horizonally. Now think of the specifics of the good luck and good fortune you'd like to attract, and choose a symbol to signify these particulars. Take one of the potato halves and hold it with the cut side facing upwards, then use a small paring knife to carefully scratch the outline of the chosen symbol into the flesh of the potato. Are you seeking greater prosperity? Carve a money sign or a pentacle. Is more love what you're after? Carve the outline of a heart into the potato. Not sure what you want, other than general good luck and good fortune? Choose a star motif, or a simple four-armed cross or other solar symbol. Just keep it simple so that the rest of the process won't be too difficult. Now that you have the outline of the symbol you want, carefully trim off the excess potato around the edges, leaving the bit with the symbol carved in it sticking up farther than the rest of the surrounding potato flesh.

Next, pour a little paint on a saucer, or find an ink pad. It's best to use something non-toxic and biodegradable; you might even experiment with all-natural "inks" like grape juice, mud, or blackberry juice. You'll also need a small piece of paper. Dip the potato into the paint or push it onto the ink pad so that the symbol is thoroughly covered in color. Think again of the good luck and good fortune you wish for, and press the potato onto the paper to stamp the symbol right at the center. Cut the symbol end off the potato half and discard, then bury the rest of the potato in the soil. If you stuck to nontoxic and biodegradable paint or ink, you can choose to rinse off as much of the stuff as possible then bury the whole potato if you prefer to bury the symbol part, as well. Hang the stamped paper in your home or carry it with you for as long as you desire.

Lughnasadh Prosperity Talisman

Talismans are magickal objects that have been in use for thousands of years. Methods for crafting talismans differ, but the basic premise is to contain a charm within a physical object, creating a magickal magnet of sorts that will draw to you whatever you seek. Words, numbers, graphic symbols, planetary correspondences, color symbolism, and other means are employed to help forge the magickal connection between talisman and whatever the talisman is designed to attract. A talisman is meant to be carried on your person, worn close to the body or tucked in a pocket so that it magnetizes your very aura with an irresistibly attractive force.

You can craft your own talisman designed especially to bring prosperity to your life this Lughnasadh season. All you'll need are a few simple items and ingredients that can be foraged from the outdoors if you don't already have them on hand.

To craft a Lughnasdh Prosperity Talisman, you'll need to first decide what material you'd like to use. Since Lughnasadh is closely associated with earth energies, you might choose to craft your talisman with clay, dough, or mud. You could use a store-bought art clay or children's play dough product, or you can make your own dough that hardens in the oven by mixing roughly two parts flour to one part salt, adding enough water to form a dough consistency, and adding a scant amount of vegetable oil a teaspoon at a time to minimize stickiness. If you're feeling primal, try crafting your talisman with mud. Look to stream banks and riverbeds for the best mud. A high clay content is ideal, but you'll be able to make do with whatever you have available. Whether using clay, dough, or mud, you'll only need a little of it; a half-cup or so will be ample.

Before you start crafting the talisman, decide if you want to incorporate any herbs or oils into its design. You might consider adding cinnamon, since it's associated with solar energies, prosperity, magickal power, and luck. You might consider adding rosemary, another solar herb that also corresponds with good luck. Add a small amount of herbs or oils to the clay, dough, or mud, and work it in with your fingers while thinking about these new energies entering into the more earthy, grounded energies of the main material.

Form the clay, dough, or mud into a small disc, roughly two to three inches in diameter. Use a toothpick or slender twig to engrave a picture of a lion into the surface of the talisman, right in the center. Lughnasadh's astrological ruler is Leo, the lion, and adding this symbol to the talisman will help synchronize your personal energy with the flow of the season so that the things you desire will be able to move towards you more freely. Above the lion, engrave an acorn, a traditional symbol of wealth and good luck. Around the lion, engrave a circle of dollar signs, apples, plus signs, or another symbol you associate with wealth and prosperity. Now think about any other symbols, words, numbers, or other images you might want to incorporate into your talisman. You might add your initials, your lucky number, the word "wealth," or any other image you feel will help attune the talisman to its purpose.

Next, place the talisman on a nonstick baking sheet, and bake in a 275-degree oven until hardened. Depending on the size and thickness of the talisman, this can take anywhere from 20–45 minutes, so keep an eye on it and take it out once it has hardened. Let the talisman cool completely before handling it.

Once it's cooled, you'll need to further empower or "charge" your talisman to fully activate it. In this stage, you are programming the finished talisman with its purpose, giving the magickal power within the object instructions for what to do. Take the talisman outside under the sun. Create a ring of coins, dollars, acorns, apples, or other symbols of wealth, and stand in the midst of this circle, talisman in hand. Let the sunbeams pour down into the talisman, and envision also the energy from the symbolic ring of wealth seeping into the talisman, charging it with the very energy it's meant to attract. Say out loud or repeat to yourself three times:

By the power of Lugh, by sun and by sky,
money and riches, to me, will they fly!

Your Lughnasadh Prosperity Talisman is now good to go; carry it with you throughout the month of August to attract greater wealth.

Lughnasadh Divination

Divination combines the use of occult tools and knowledge with the power of observation to allow easier access to the collective consciousness and to your own inner intuition and psychic abilities. Like the spells above, the following divination methods can be successfully used at any time, but may be more effective if used during the month of August. Trust your senses, and be open to the information and feelings that come to you.

Traditional Methods of Foretelling the Weather

The art of divining the weather is nearly lost in modern times, but this long-standing tradition still holds its roots in many places. August weather lore abounds, so why not practice a little weather prophecy of your own this season? In North Carolina, Kentucky, Alabama, New York, and Oklahoma, for instance, common folk belief holds that the number of fogs in August predicts the number of snows that will occur during the coming winter. Elsewhere in America, it was said that if August was dry and arid, the safety of the harvest need not be feared. American weather prophets even consulted with the insects to form their predictions; it was believed that the louder the sound of the katydids in August, the bigger the blizzards come December.

Weather lore was common in Europe, as well. A proverb attributed to the *Book of Knowledge*, a nineteenth-century children's encyclopedia, warns that thunder in August signifies a year of sickness and sadness. In Albania, it was believed that the first twelve days of August presaged the weather for the coming twelve months (Swainson, 119–121). In parts of England, the weather on August 24, St. Bartholomew's Day, was said to be indicative of the weather for the entire autumn, while if there was good weather on August 15, St. Mary's Day, a fine wine harvest was predicted. It was thought that if August brought warm sunshine and bright stars, the grapes could be expected to ripen well. If August was cold following a hot July, a cold and dry winter was presaged. In Scotland, rain at Lammas meant a fruitful harvest, while rain after Lammas was undesirable (Binney).

Traditional Corn Divination

As a harvest celebration, the Lughnasadh sabbat is often associated with vegetables and grains such as corn. In both Mexico and the United States, corn has long been used as a tool for foretelling the future. One method is to place thirty kernels of dried corn in a bowl, concentrate on a yes or no question for which you'd like to know the answer, then grab a handful of kernels out of the dish. Move the remaining kernels to the side, and divide the handful of kernels you picked out into equal piles of four kernels each, setting any leftover kernels to the side separately. Now count your piles. If you have an even number of piles, and an even number of leftover kernels, the answer to your question is yes. If you instead have an odd number of piles and an odd number of leftover kernels, the answer to your question is no. If you have an even number of piles but an odd number of leftover kernels, it signifies that the powers refuse to make an answer (Cunningham, 52–53).

Another method of corn divination from Mexico is used to help diagnose disease and illness. A handful of corn kernels are cast onto a cloth, or are placed in a bowl of water and swirled around. The final arrangement of kernels are then interpreted to give an indication of the patient's health and well-being (Austin and Lujan, 248). If the kernels are evenly distributed, it signifies that a full recovery might be expected. If the kernels are instead clumped together in certain areas, it's a sign that trouble may be brewing in the corresponding area of the body. You might select the top of the bowl or cloth to represent the head, the bottom of the bowl or cloth to represent the feet, the sides to represent the extremities, and the center to represent the internal organs. However, please keep in mind that while this divination method might indeed provide relevant clues to a person's general state of health, it's no substitute for a traditional diagnosis by a qualified medical professional.

Water Scrying Divination to Predict Success

As summer continues to wane and autumn grows steadily closer, many of us become more introspective and thoughtful, and a mood of reflection and retrospection often takes us. When we're in this state of mind, images and information from the subconscious become more accessible. One way to tap into the hidden wisdom of your subconscious and check on the progress of your goals is through a form of divination known as scrying. Scrying involves gazing steadily with relaxed eyes into a surface until the mind enters into a hypnotic and psychically aware state. Visions are perceived and information is received by the subconscious mind, which then conveys this knowledge to the conscious mind and/or to other people present for the scrying session. We magickal folks all operate differently, and for some of us, once we enter a trance state, our conscious mind completely checks out. We might have an awesomely successful scrying session only to find that when we come back to our regular state of mind, all we learned and experienced in the scrying session is completely forgotten. For others, our conscious mind and subconscious mind are meshed together so thoroughly that we seldom let go of either one completely, and even when we do, we're able to retain memories of the things experienced and witnessed in varying mental states of conscious awareness and subconscious trance. If you fall into the first camp, it's a good idea to have someone with you while you scry to act as note-taker and witness to the information you convey while emerged in the psychic state. If there's no one to join you, consider using an audio recorder to capture any gems of wisdom or visions you utter out while entranced.

Perform this divination on Autumn Eve for best results. Find a large, wide bowl, preferably black in color and ceramic. If you can't find a black bowl, blacken it with waterproof paint.

Fill the bowl with water. If you live near the ocean or near a relatively unpolluted river, stream, or lake, you might use water from these sources in your divination bowl.

Put the divination bowl on a table or on the floor. Make the room as dark as is safe and comfortable for you. You don't want to go bumping into things, but you also don't want bright, glaring light; find your own comfortable compromise. Light a single candle, and hold this for a moment over the divination bowl so the flame is reflected in the water. Think of the metaphorical "seeds" you've planted, your plans and projects, the hopes, fears, and energies you project, then say out loud or to yourself:

Fire burn and water glow,
show me what I need to know!
Seeds I planted, seeds I sowed,
tell me, will my garden grow?

Place the candle to the side so that the flame is no longer visible on the water's surface. Take a few slow breaths until you feel calm and centered, then gaze into the water. Blink as you normally do and relax your eyes. Don't try to focus, but merely gaze passively at your reflection, as a casual yet interested and curious observer. Before long, the image in the water will start to morph. You may see a double image, a blurry image, or a moving image, or your reflection might disappear completely. When this happens, it's startling if we're not expecting it, and the feeling of surprise can wrench us back to conscious reality quickly, which is not what we want when trying to enter into a psychic mindset. However the reflection in the water happens to morph, do your best to keep watching, as this is a signal that the good stuff is about to begin. The water will eventually turn a solid color (often a celestial blue or solid black), then specks of light will appear, eventually clearing to submerge the scryer completely in a mental state of psychic awareness. Everyone experiences scrying visions differently. You might witness images playing across the surface of the water like a movie on a screen. You might find that the images and information simply enter your mind and you experience these visions as if you're daydreaming. You might feel like you're transported to the actual scene of the vision, much like it feels when we're dreaming in a deep sleep. Keep an open mind and don't try to interpret your visions and impressions as they come to you; utter out loud what you see and sense, then worry about interpreting this information once you come back to normal, non-trance reality.

What did you experience? Write down any further thoughts, and evaluate the impressions collected during the scrying session via note-taker or audio recorder. Remember that as a Lughnasadh-themed divination session, the initial intention was set on the idea of harvest. Did your scrying visions give you a clearer idea of what you can expect to reap from the seeds you have sown? Were the impressions generally positive? If so, you can expect a good "harvest" or return on the metaphorical seeds you've planted. Were the impressions challenging or negative? If so, you might want to give your plans and projects a little extra love, effort, and attention to help overcome any looming obstacles foreseen on the horizon.

Pendulum Divination to Identify Dangers

Lughnasadh is a traditional time to work protection magick for crops, livestock, and other valuables. If you plan to do some protective spellwork of your own this season, it might benefit you to know exactly where your magickal efforts are most needed. A pendulum offers a simple means of divination that can help you determine the relative safety of your various personal possessions, enabling you to anticipate potential danger and thus focus your protective magick right where it's needed most.

First, think of the valuables you wish to protect. Start with the major ones. Do you have a home? A car? Fancy jewelry or art? Sentimental items? Crops or gardens? Pets or livestock? Pendulum in hand, stand in front of each one. Hold the pendulum in your right hand between your thumb and forefinger so that it swings over the open, flat palm of your left hand. Ask the pendulum if the possession in question is likely to encounter danger in the coming months. Don't direct the pendulum; hold it as still as possible. It should begin to move on its own, either spinning around in a circle or swinging back and forth in a straight line. If it spins in a circle, the pendulum's answer is affirmative. If it moves in a back and forth line, the answer is no. If the pendulum indicates that any of your property is in need of extra protection, casting some preventative defensive magick can help ward off the danger and help ensure the safety of your possessions.

RECIPES
AND
CRAFTS

on, introspection, discernment, sacrifice, excellent time for magic

y, abundance, strength, growth, protection, honoring ancestors,

formation, or communication with the dead, sacred wells, hill

for magick, astronomical midpoint between the Summer Sol

at 15 degrees Leo in the Northern Hemisphere, Sun at

arius in the Southern Hemisphere, Mother Goddess, Earth

Goddess, water nymphs, tree nymphs, the spirit of the land,

Earth God, Solar God, the warrior, the protector, the sac

e dying god, the spirit of vegetation, the newly crowned king,

Dryads, Demeter, Kore, Evannetar, Nemesis, Ops, Va

Juturna, Stata Mater, Danu, Artemis, Ceres, Lug

htli, Consus, Thor, Vulcan, Thoth, Loki, Vertumnus, Of

r energies, happiness, transformation. Brown: Earth energies,

llumination, success, divine power, harvest Green: Abundance

vegetation Herb Blackberry: Protection, binding, defense, ob

healing, abundance, friendship, love Allspice: Money, wealth,

agickal power Basil: Protection, luck, love, wealth, abundance

Solar energies, healing, protection, friendship, peace, prospera

WHILE FORMAL LUGHNASADH rituals and magick workings are very satisfying, so too is incorporating the celebration of the sabbat into the more mundane aspects of our everyday lives. Through cooking, crafts, and decorating, we can more fully experience the uniqueness and joy of the special time we call Lughnasadh. In this chapter, you'll find ideas for recipes, crafts, and décor to help you celebrate Lughnasadh in style.

Recipes

Lughnasadh is a holiday celebrating the summer harvest, and cooking with in-season vegetables and herbs will really help you tune in and connect to this sabbat's energy flow. We're glad for the harvest but miserable from the continuing heat, and there's nothing like a stacked plate of wholesome food to help dampen the misery and increase feelings of gladness and gratitude. Try cooking with summer squash, beans, corn, and leafy greens, and serve up lots of fresh bilberries, blueberries, and apples to go along with it. Seasonal herbs include basil, oregano, rosemary, and garlic—try incorporating these spices to give your recipes a little dose of Lughnasadh harvest flair. Bread is also an important component of Lughnasadh culinary fare; try baking a loaf or two to complement your Lughnasadh meals. Choose foods that are hearty, but not too heavy or spicy as to be overwhelming in the late summer heat. Here's a menu to try that's just right for a casual Lughnasadh get-together with friends or family:

On the Menu:

- Vegetable Bean Soup for Celebration
- Roasted Sacrificial Corn God on the Cob
- Satisfying Squash Casserole
- Nurturing Apple Tart
- Blessed Bread
- Spicy Goddess Apple Cider

Vegetable Bean Soup for Celebration

This recipe celebrates the harvest by including a variety of fresh and hearty vegetables. When possible, use locally grown, organic produce. It's okay to substitute or leave out any ingredients you don't have.

You'll Need:

1 pound of cooked dried black beans or one 16-ounce can of black beans

1 pound of cooked dried dark red kidney beans or one 16-ounce can of dark red kidney beans

1 pound of cooked dried garbanzo beans or one 16-ounce can of garbanzo beans

1 pound of fresh green beans or one 16-ounce can of green beans

1 small onion

3 small tomatoes, chopped, or one 16-ounce can of stewed, diced tomatoes

4 medium-sized potatoes, washed (but not peeled) and chopped into 1-inch chunks

2 cups broccoli, chopped

3 large carrots, diced

1 bunch of kale, washed and chopped with stalk ends removed

1 clove of garlic, crushed and minced

1 teaspoon salt
1 teaspoon black pepper
1 teaspoon oregano
1 teaspoon basil

Prepare the ingredients and place everything in a large pot. Cover with enough water to fill the pot. Heat over medium-low for about an hour, stirring occasionally. As you stir the soup, let the aromas fill you, and think about the variety and loveliness of each ingredient you've added to the mix. Smile widely, and direct this cheerful energy out through the spoon in your hand and into the soup. Once it's ready, share the soup with friends while enjoying happy conversation and celebrating the good things the waning summer has brought.

Roasted Sacrificial Corn God on the Cob

Corn is a very traditional Lughnasadh food, symbolic of the harvest and an embodiment of the necessary and inescapable death of the crops once they're harvested. Some Pagan traditions include paying homage to a corn god who dies at this time of year, a representative of all the other plants in the field who give their lives for the sake and nourishment of humankind. This easy recipe acts as a reminder of the earth's great sacrifice, the vegetables and grains that die for our own sustenance.

You'll Need:
Corn on the cob, preferably fresh with husks still attached
butter
salt
black pepper

Start with whole, fresh corn on the cob if possible. If it has the husks still on it, all the better; leave them on and simply place the corn in a 350° oven for about 30 minutes. If you're cooking on a grill, remove a few layers of the outermost husks but leave most of the husks intact. Place the corn over red-hot coals and turn frequently for about fifteen minutes, until the outer husks are charred. If the corn has already been husked, wrap the ears in aluminum foil and roast or grill them in the same way. Once the corn is done, peel back the husks if there are any, or unwrap the foil. Spread on a pat of butter and sprinkle with salt (symbolic of the sun's energy) and black pepper (symbolic of death). Eat while thinking of all the plants that die each year at harvest, and the humans and other animals that continue to live because of this.

Satisfying Squash Casserole

This squash casserole will help relieve the feelings of angst and insatiability that often plague us during August's dog days. Use it to promote feelings of gratitude and temper irritability.

You'll Need:
5 to 7 medium-sized yellow crookneck or straightneck
　　squash—sometimes called summer squash
1 medium-sized yellow onion, diced
1 clove garlic, crushed and minced
1 cup shredded cheddar cheese
4 tablespoons of butter
1 teaspoon salt
½ teaspoon black pepper
3 to 4 large eggs

Begin by holding each piece of squash in your hand in turn, thinking of something that frustrates you or leaves you feeling unsatisfied, and sending these feelings out through your hand and into the squash. Sense the emotional energy of your frustrations and agitations flowing through you and out of you; visualize the energy as an orange-tinted light if you're having trouble feeling it. Wash the squash, visualizing your frustrations lying at the bottom of a river bed where they'll be transformed by the force of rushing water. Next, cut off the stem ends of the squash and discard them. Don't peel the squash. Cut each piece into 1"-thick discs, then place them in a pot of water. Bring the water to a boil, and as it heats, think of the heat outdoors, and think of your own desires and points of dissatisfaction flowing out of the squash and into the water, increasing in intensity as the contents of the pot get hotter. Boil the squash for about 7 minutes, until it's tender. If it's easy to pierce the squash with the prongs of a fork, it's ready. If you need to apply a lot of pressure to get the fork to go in, let the squash boil for a few more minutes. Once it's ready, drain the water through a colander and set the squash aside to cool, leaving it in the strainer for the time being.

In the meantime, melt the butter in a small pan, then add the onion and garlic, then the salt and pepper.

Sauté just until the onions start to become translucent and the fragrance from the garlic has intensified. As you sauté the mixture, think of the energetic vibrations of the onion and garlic, both vegetables associated with strength and courage. Breathe in the scent as they cook, letting it fill your body with a strong, courageous energy. You are tough enough to overcome any frustration. Turn off the heat, and place the pan to the side to cool as you turn your attention back to the squash.

Now that it's cooled enough to handle, press the squash with your hands or a small saucer, squeezing as much water out as possible. As you do so, envision any lingering frustrations or agitations you still have being squeezed out as well. Now mash the squash a bit with the back of a fork, imagining that you are grinding your frustrated energies down into the dirt, smashing any unsatisfied or agitated feelings into oblivion. You don't have to mash the squash too much, just enough so that it's a pulpy mixture rather than large, solid chunks.

Dump the squash into a mixing bowl and stir in the eggs then the flour, blending thoroughly after each ingredient is added. Flour and egg both have stabilizing energies, so as you mix them into the squash, envision the energies in the bowl taking on a steady, calm vibration. Breath slowly and deeply as you stir. Next add the onion and garlic, imagining an energy of strength and courage entering into the blend as you mix. Will this energy to enter into yourself as well, visualizing the power in the garlic and onion swirling throughout the bowl, up through the spoon, and into your body, infusing you with increased strength and courage. Stand tall and proud, as if you were a roaring, courageous lion or other fearsome beast.

Finally, stir in most of the cheese, reserving about ¼ cup. As you mix, fix your face into an expression of utter contentment and do your best to feign an attitude of absolute satisfaction. Give your best performance and try to really *feel* the role, as if you were a great actor. Fill your head with thoughts about your blessings and the good things in life. Speak to yourself about how you're totally satisfied in all facets of life, even if this is not really the case. To put it simply, make believe! With your happiest smile, pour the mixture into an oven-safe dish, and top with the remaining cheese. Bake at 400 degrees for 15 minutes, then reduce heat to 350 and bake for an additional 30 minutes, or until the casserole seems solid and the cheese on top is melted and golden brown. While it cooks, treat yourself to some fun time, doing something you truly enjoy, whether it's chilling out listening to your favorite music, reading a book, painting a picture, or playing a video game. Do something purely for the sake of your own entertainment. When the casserole has finished cooking, let it cool for 5–10 minutes, then enjoy as a side dish. Feelings of irritability, agitation, and dissatisfaction will be greatly reduced, making room for gratitude. Think about or chat about the things in your life you're happy about and grateful for as you eat.

Nurturing Apple Tart

This sweet dessert is magickally blended with nurturing, loving energies to help all who eat it tune in to the energies of Mother Earth. At this time of year when the fruits in Nature's bursting belly are ripening in earnest, we too can grow to our full potentials. The magickal power of this Nurturing Apple Tart will help you feel good enough to do just that.

You'll Need:

TART SHELL

1 cup all-purpose flour

¼ cup sugar

⅛ teaspoon salt

½ teaspoon vanilla powder or cinnamon (optional)

3 to 4 tablespoons cold water

6 tablespoons butter, softened and cut into ½-inch cubes

FILLING

4 medium apples, washed and peeled (save the cores!)

2 tablespoons sugar

½ teaspoon cinnamon

several small pats of butter

GLAZE

Apple cores reserved from the apples you're using, along with
several apple slices

¼ cup sugar

¾ cup water (approximate; will vary depending on the size
    and quantity of your apple chunks)

For the tart shell, stir together 1 cup all-purpose flour, ¼ cup
sugar, and ⅛ teaspoon salt. If desired, add ½ teaspoon of vanilla powder or cinnamon at this time, blending it into the
flour until evenly mixed and conjuring a feeling of love in your
heart as you do so. Cut in 2 tablespoons butter, sliced into ½
inch cubes. Mash the butter into the flour using the back of a
fork or a pastry blender. Blend it until it's nice and crumbly, almost like a very course corn meal or moist sand type texture.
Add in 4 more tablespoons butter (also cut into ½ inch cubes),
this time mixing them in with your hands. To best incorporate
the butter into the flour, get your hands down in the flour and
butter cubes, pinch it together a little bit at a time between
your fingertips, and make a sort of twisting motion with your
hands to mash it all together. The key is to not mash it too
much. You'll want to just barely work it in, leaving pea-sized
chunks in the butter/flour mix. Using your hands is impera-
tive, as it's far too easy to over blend with a machine or utensil.
As you blend in the butter, think of the mixture in the bowl as
the earth, and think of the butter as the effort and energy expended by humans and nature alike in order for the harvest to
come to bloom. Next, drizzle in several tablespoons of water,

adding a little at a time while thinking of the rains that help nourish the land. Slowly and gently toss the mixture in your hands until it starts to come together. Softly press the dough together until it forms a ball, flatten it a bit, then place it in the refrigerator to chill for about 30 minutes.

While the dough chills, prepare the apples by peeling, coring, and slicing them into ¼–½ inch thick wedges. As you handle the apples, think of how wonderful the fruit is—such a common fruit, yet so beautiful, delicious, and nourishing. Send a feeling of love and gratitude into the apples, focusing your mind on something that makes you feel happy, grateful, or loved as you make each cut. Save the apple cores and place them in a small saucepan along with a few of the apple slices. Add just enough water to the saucepan to cover the apple pieces, and leave it be for now.

After the dough has chilled, place it on a well-floured surface and roll it out to an ⅛-inch thickness. Put a sprinkling of flour on top of the dough and your rolling pin so it won't stick. Once flattened, roll the dough around the rolling pin then unroll it into a lightly greased 9-inch tart pan (any oven-proof pan or baking dish will do, really), letting the edges overlap the sides of the pan. Fill the middle with apple slices, then sprinkle on 2 tablespoons of sugar and ½ teaspoon cinnamon. Place several small pats of butter on the top of the apples, about 2 to 3 inches apart. Fold the sides of the dough in over the apples toward the center of the dish, overlapping, pinching, and trimming where needed. The dough won't reach all the way to the middle of the dish, and there should be a circle of apples left uncovered in the center. It doesn't need to look perfect at all, and in fact, a uniquely shaped crust gives the tart a nice rustic feel.

Bake in a preheated oven at 350 degrees for 40 to 45 minutes, until the crust is crispy and golden. Let it cool for about 10 minutes. While you wait, turn your attention to the apple pieces you previously placed in a saucepan covered with a bit of water. Heat it over medium, slowly stirring and adding in ¼ cup of sugar and ½ teaspoon cinnamon. Let this mixture simmer for several minutes until it starts to thicken into a syrup-like consistency, then turn off the heat. Fish out the chunks of apple using a spoon or fork, then let the glaze cool slightly. Brush the top of the tart with the apple cinnamon glaze and enjoy!

Blessed Bread

This simple and traditional Irish soda bread is ideal for sabbat offerings or as a tasty and magickal addition to your holiday meals. This bread will help bring good health and good fortune to all who receive it or eat it.

You'll need:
3 cups all-purpose flour
1½ teaspoons baking soda
1½ cups buttermilk

Mix together the flour and baking soda, thinking of the growing grain, the sun, the land, and the harvest as you stir the ingredients. Slowly add the buttermilk, working it in gently until the mixture develops into a soft and clumpy dough. Don't over-stir or be too rough with the dough or it will become overly stiff and dense. Form the dough into a disc about 6 inches or so in diameter; the disc should be rounded on top and a couple of inches thick in the middle. Place the dough on a lightly greased or floured baking sheet. Using a knife, make an indention of a large "x" or cross shape in the top surface of the dough, extending out not quite to the edges of the disc. As you mark the symbol, think of the protective forces and energies that help sustain the earth and its lifeforms, and say a short prayer for blessings using your own words or these:

May the gods bless the bread, and may we be blessed!

Bake the bread in a preheated oven at 400 degrees for around 20 to 30 minutes. You'll know the bread is ready once it's hardened and slightly browned on top. Cool the loaf and break off pieces to share and enjoy.

Spicy Goddess Apple Cider

This cider will help infuse those who drink it with a loving energy just right for connecting with the goddess spirit. It can be served hot or cold.

You'll need:
2 quarts apple cider
1 cinnamon stick or 1 teaspoon powdered cinnamon
1 vanilla bean or ½ teaspoon vanilla extract
1 small orange and 3 large strawberries
2 tablespoons sugar

Pour the apple cider into a large pot, and begin simmering it over medium-low heat. As you wait for it to heat up, cut the orange into circular slices, and cut the strawberries into halves. Add the sugar to the apple cider and blend thoroughly, then add the fruit pieces, the vanilla bean (scored along one side) or vanilla extract, and the cinnamon stick or powdered cinnamon. Stir the mixture every now and then using a slow, clockwise rotation. As the cider heats, think of the energies within the fruit and spices flowing into the liquid, infusing it with energies of love, beauty, passion, and joy. Heat to a steaming simmer, but don't let the mixture boil. Remove the fruit pieces. Enjoy the cider hot or cold, and know that it will fill you with the light of the goddess whenever you drink it.

Crafts

There's nothing like a sabbat to get us feeling extra crafty! Here are some simple crafts to make and use this Lughnasadh season.

Corn Silk Blessing Wand

This easy-to-make magickal tool is great for blessing your fellow Lughnasadh ritualists. Infused with the power of the Corn Spirit, a touch from a Corn Silk Blessing Wand will invite energies of strength, fertility, and prosperity to enter.

You'll Need:
stick, 6–9 inches long
one ear of fresh corn, husks attached
yellow thread

Begin by selecting an ear of fresh corn that seems especially attractive or healthy. Peel back the husks about halfway, and wrap your hand around the lower portion of the corn. Sense the energies within the vegetable, and use visualization and intention to will these energies out of the cob and into the corn silk that surrounds it. Think of the spirit of the corn, not just in the piece that you hold in your hand, but in all the corn that grows around the world. Imagine this energy flowing first into the corn ear and then back out, magnified, into the corn silk. Finish removing the husks, then trim off the tassel of corn silk at the top of the cob.

Next, choose a stick about 6 to 9 inches long to serve as the main body of the wand. Make sure the stick is pliable and/or green inside; a "wispy" wand will serve you best. Don't clean it—if earth clings to the stick, then all the better, as soil makes a perfect accompaniment for the powerful fertile energies embodied by the corn plant. Using a short length of yellow string, attach the tassel of corn silk to the top of the wand, tying it on about an inch and a half down from the tip.

Corn Silk Blessing Wand

Your Corn Silk Blessing Wand is now ready for use. Lightly brush the corn silk tip over the arms, hands, faces, or other body parts of your ritualists to infuse them with the blessings of the Corn Spirit and increase their feelings of strength, energy, and well-being. This tool can also be used to bless other tools, as well. Just brush it over the surface of any ritual implement to give the tool a dash of Lughnasadh flair and magickal power. It can also be used as a miniature ritual broom; use it to sweep off the surface of your altar before beginning your Lughnasadh rites.

Multi-Purpose Magickal Berry Ink

Gorgeous, colorful, and packed with magickal energy, many berries ripen and become ready to pick near Lammastide. Here's a recipe for a berry-powered magickal ink that can be used in a variety of seasonal charms and rituals.

You'll Need:
fresh berries (blackberry, bilberry, raspberry, or blueberry)
sturdy bowl and heavy glass, or mortar and pestle
gauzy fabric (cheesecloth, muslin, or lace) or a fine wire
    mesh strainer
toothpick
small paintbrush or twig

You'll need one to two cups of fresh berries, depending on how much ink you want to make. You can make a tiny amount of ink with just a few berries if that's all you have, but if you've got plenty of berries, it's best if you use at least a cup so that you'll have plenty of end product to work with. You can use a variety of berries in your ink, or stick with just one type. Try to find pesticide-free, locally grown or wild berries— blackberries, bilberries, raspberries, and blueberries all work nicely. The riper and darker the berries, the more pigmented and potent the ink.

Wash the berries in cool water, and pour them into a sturdy bowl. Crush them with the bottom of a heavy glass or cup; if you have a mortar and pestle, use that. As you smash and crush the berries, think about the qualities you'd like the magickal ink to have. You might formulate the ink for protection, thinking of the prickly thorns or pointy leaves of the plants on which the berries grew and envisioning the defensive energies in the berries welling up, magnified and powerful enough to repel any danger. You might instead want to craft an ink for prosperity; mash the berries as you think of their sweet and plentiful juices running freely, abundantly. Perhaps you want to be able to use the ink for a variety of purposes. If that's the case, think of each and every quality you wish to bring out in the berries as you crush them. Berries contain energies attuned with love, prosperity, protection, passion, and happiness—just think of the specific vibration you desire increasing in magnitude until all the berries are brimming with that particular energetic quality.

Once the berries are mashed, you'll need to strain out the juice that will soon become your magickal ink. A gauzy fabric like cheesecloth, muslin, or even lace will work great, or you can use a fine wire mesh strainer. If you don't have any of these items, a coffee filter will work in a pinch. Place the berries in the strainer or bundle them up in the cloth or coffee filter, then squeeze, collecting the juice in a bowl. Squeeze as much juice out of the berries as possible. After you've pressed out all the liquid, discard the solid berry parts, and turn your attention to the resulting juice. Use a toothpick to slowly swirl the juice around the bowl as you say:

Infused with the powers of earth and sun,
what's written with this ink will surely be won!

Now that your magickal ink is complete, it's time to use it. Dip a small paintbrush, twig, or toothpick into the berry ink, then use it to draw a symbol of your intentions on a slip of paper. You might draw a pentacle for protection, a dollar sign for prosperity, or a heart for love and passion. You can also use the ink as a body paint—try decorating your hands, arms, face, or chest with berry ink before or during your Lammastide rituals to give your personal magickal power and vital energy a boost. You can even use the ink as an edible paint; brush it in the shape of words or symbols on top of frosted cakes, cupcakes, or cookies for a dash of extra magick.

Corn Dolly

Residents in England in the late sixteenth century liked to make little figures out of corn leaves at harvest time. These magical charms were thought to protect the home, livestock, and personal health alike. Here's how to make a corn dolly or "kirn baby" to help ensure protection and good luck for your home, self, or property this Lughnasadh and beyond.

You'll Need:
corn husks
scissors
dull pencil, marker, or burnt matchstick

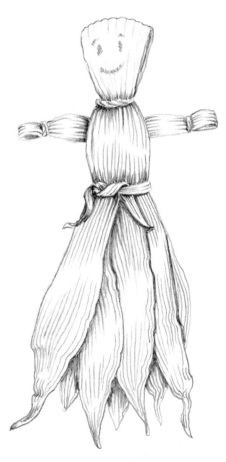

Corn Dolly

You'll need an ear of corn for each dolly. Peel the husks off the cob. Find the largest husk, and fold it in half from top to bottom so you'll have a loop at the top, and two ends hanging loose at the bottom. To start giving your corn dolly shape, form the head and legs—tear off a small strip from another corn husk, and tie it about an inch below the top loop of the husk you've folded in half. That loop becomes the head, and the two ends hanging loose at the bottom become the legs. Next, choose a slender leaf to form the arms of your dolly. Lay it flat and place the dolly right in the center. Fold each end of the "arm husk" in towards the center, overlapping the ends slightly. Tear off a long strip from another corn husk, and tie it around the center of the doll's "waist" to secure the arms in place. Add more corn husk as desired. You might tie small pieces around the end of each arm to make hands. You might attach narrow strips of corn husks, or silky strands of corn silk, to the head of your dolly to give it a patch of hair. You might even use some of the extra corn husks to make clothing for your corn dolly; a husk wrapped horizontally around the waist of your doll makes a nice mini-skirt, while a row of overlapping corn husks arranged vertically and attached with a slender corn husk "belt" becomes a long, full skirt. Finally, add a face to your corn dolly, drawing on the features using a dull pencil, a permanent marker, or the charred end of a burnt matchstick. Place the dolly in the sun to dry, then hang it in your home, place it somewhere around your property, or carry it on your person to help obtain magickal protection and encourage good luck.

Décor

Decorating for Lughnasadh takes a little more creativity and attention to details than decorating for some of the other sabbats. Lughnasadh is sort of an in-between holiday, rife with harvest themes most often associated in modern times with autumn, but occurring smack-dab in the middle of summer according to our standard reckonings of the seasons. We have Mabon at the Autumn Equinox to celebrate fall and the harvest, and we have Litha at the Summer Solstice to celebrate the sunshine and the summer. Lughnasadh falls right in the middle and shares common themes with both holidays. So how do you make your Lughnasadh decorating stand out from your Mabon or Litha decorating? The secret to capturing Lughnasadh's subtle nuances is in the details. Think along the lines of what's specific to Lughnasadh, and then highlight what makes the holiday special by adding accents to your home's décor. For example, since Lughnasadh is often seen as a celebration of the year's first major harvest, you might find out which fruits and vegetables are in season in your local area and create a simple centerpiece featuring some of these local "first fruits." As another idea, you might choose to create a special altar dedicated especially to the Celtic god Lugh.

Since summer's heat and insatiable sunshine still linger in most places this time of year, you'll want to save your heavier fabrics and deeper color schemes for Mabon, but you can still add in a few hints of the cooler autumn season that's bound to come. Try textured fabrics in the form of fuzzy throw pillows or embroidered curtains to incorporate that homey, comfy feeling of harvest time without making the look too heavy for summer. Choose a mix of pale and bold colors, incorporating different shades of golds, yellows, and oranges into your holiday decorations. Here are a few specific ideas to try that will have your home looking festive for the season.

Apple Invasion!

Nothing brings to mind the atmosphere of the early August country fair better than a bushel of fresh apples and the scent of sweet fruit in the air. Why not invite the magick of apples into your home this Lughnasadh by featuring them prominently in your décor? These colorful and edible decorations can help create an ambiance with a laid-back and comfortable yet festive and vibrant feel. Place a large bushel of apples in the corner of a room, and place smaller bowls of apples on tables and counter tops. You can even skip the bowl, and stack apples in a pyramid formation or other creative arrangement.

Apples come in many sizes and colors, and you can combine these into different arrangements to create various effects. Play around with various apples, including green, golden, red apples, and pink varieties, and find the combinations that most appeal to you. You can further amplify the apple-themed ambience by using apple-scented incense or potpourri. Or, infuse your home with apple scent the old-fashioned and delicious way, by making up a batch of hot apple cider or baking a fresh apple pie.

Gratitude Altar

Lughnasadh is traditionally a time to give thanks for our blessings and express gratitude for the people and powers who helped us along the way. A Gratitude Altar can act as a powerful place to do just that, in addition to doubling as a festive focal point in your holiday décor. Your Gratitude Altar is meant to be highly personalized, but here's the basic set-up:

Begin by placing an altar cloth on top of a small table you will use for your altar. You might choose a gold cloth to represent success and gratitude, a red cloth to represent energy and sacrifice, or another color that feels right to you. Stand before the empty altar now and take a moment to think about all the effort and energy you've been expending over the course of the summer, and think about what you've gained from those efforts. Perhaps you're a gardener and your summer labors have brought in a nice harvest of squash. Perhaps you're a city witch, and the work you've been doing at the local homeless shelter has been spiritually rewarding. Keep in mind that success doesn't necessarily come in dollars and cents and piles of jewels; sometimes success is subtle but if we're able to notice it, even the smallest successes tend to multiply. Whether your summertime harvest has brought in a bushel of apples or an influx of creative energy and inspiration, if you think about it, you're sure to find at least some measure of success for which you're grateful. Did anyone or anything else play a role in this success? As we rejoice in the fruits of our summer labors, we also recognize the roles others have played in making those fruits a reality. As you stand before your altar, make a mental list of not only your blessings but also of the people and powers who helped to bestow or preserve those blessings.

Next, look through your house for objects you could use to represent the various items on your mental list of gratitude. For instance, are you thankful for the love and support of your children or your parents? If so, gather some photos of these special people, and place the photos on your Gratitude Altar. Did you get a new job or a raise, and are you grateful to have a little more spending money? Place a coin or dollar on the altar, in addition to a business card or other implement to represent your place of employment. Gather as many items as you like, and place them on your altar.

Next, choose a symbol of your own feelings of gratitude to place on the altar, something along the lines of an offering or gift. Fresh, seasonal fruits or vegetables are a great choice. You might even place your offerings inside a cornucopia, a traditional symbol of abundance. Infuse the offering with your love and gratitude by holding it in your hands and expressing your heartfelt emotions, sending the energy out through your palms or fingertips and directing it into the offering. Place the offering on the altar.

Finally, decide on a simple ritual you can do at least once a day at your Gratitude Altar, something to further express your thanks to the people and powers that have helped you gain success. You might light a candle and meditate for a few moments, or simply pause beside the altar and say a quick thanks! For something a little more elaborate, consider composing a song or verse you could sing or recite, or perhaps even choreograph a dance routine to perform. Are you an artist? If so, you might create miniature works of art to place on your altar as additional offerings to your special helpers. If baking is more your talent, consider baking up a fresh loaf of bread to share at the altar.

Choose something personal, something that means something to you and conveys your own tastes or talents. Whatever you choose, do this additional ritual at your Gratitude Altar as much as possible throughout the week leading up to Lughnasadh and throughout the remainder of the month of August. Keep your altar clean and free of dust or clutter, removing any expired food offerings in proper course and freshening up the space with a dust cloth or altar broom as necessary.

Hanging Sunbursts

This simple craft uses corn husks and natural dye made from blueberries to create a colorful hanging ornament reminiscent of the sun and just right for Lughnasadh's solar and harvest themes. You'll need about fifteen dried corn husks for each sunburst, some twine or heavy string, and a pound or so of blueberries. Begin by placing the blueberries in a large pot and add water in a two to one ratio. For instance, if you use one cup of blueberries, you'll need two cups of water. Bring the mixture to a boil, then reduce heat and simmer for about an hour. Allow the mixture to cool, and strain out the blueberries using a colander, collecting the liquid in a large container. Pour the dye mixture into a shallow bowl or deep tray, and into this, submerge the corn husks. The corn husks will float, so you will need to weigh them down with a can of food or a heavy plate. Leave them in the dye overnight, then hang the husks on a clothesline, or lay them out on newspapers or place them in the grass to dry. Be sure to separate the corn husks so that they'll all dry thoroughly. The result will be a collection of corn husks tinted a purplish, deep mauve shade.

Hanging Sunbursts

Now take about fifteen of these husks and place them in a stack, one on top of the other. Your corn husks will be narrower on one end, so alternate the layers to make sure your finished sunburst looks symmetrical. Tie the corn husks together at the middle using a piece of heavy string or twine. Leave a length of string attached so you can hang up the sunburst once it's complete. What you have now should look roughly like a bow-tie shape. Next, start separating the corn husks, bending the ends of the husks in towards the center of the "bow-tie," creating a V shape. Continue bending the husks in this manner, reversing the direction of the V once you're about halfway through the stack of husks to create a pompom effect. Split the corn husks as you go to make narrower ribbons and to give the sunburst a fuller look. Once it's complete, hang the sunburst in a sunny window, suspend it over the dinner table, or place it anywhere you need to add a dash of Lughnasadh pizazz.

Farm Furnishings

You can also jazz up your yard with some Lughnasadh flair, too. Consider farming and gardening themes for an easy way to decorate using objects you probably already have. Dig up all your old gardening tools or farming equipment, and place these in conspicuous places around your yard: a shovel planted by the mailbox, a wheelbarrow resting in front of the old oak tree, a watering can sitting beside the front door. Fill unused plant pots with soil, put them in a row on your front porch, and place a basket of seed packets and a pair of gardening gloves beside it, inviting your visitors to be your guests in doing some planting. Scatter some hay on the ground. Obtain pumpkins or gourds and arrange them in small groupings here and there around your property. You might even want to fashion a scarecrow—stuff a set of old clothes with rags or newspaper, create a face by stuffing a pillowcase and painting on an expression, tie it all together so that it's shaped like a human, and hang it on a tall pole or broomstick you've stuck vertically into the ground. Your yard will look like a harvest landscape in no time.

PRAYERS
AND
INVOCATIONS

...on, introspection, discernment, sacrifice, excellent time for magic... abundance, strength, growth, protection, honoring ancestors... formation, or communications with the dead, sacred wells, hel... for magick, astronomical midpoint between the Summer Sol... at 15 degrees Leo in the Northern Hemisphere, Sun at... ...arius in the Southern Hemisphere, Mother Goddess, Earth... Goddess, water nymphs, tree nymphs, the spirit of the land... Earth God, Solar God, the warrior, the protector, the sac... ...e dying god, the spirit of vegetation, the newly crowned king... Dryads, Demeter, Kore, Swannotar, Nemesis, Ops, Ha... Juturna, Stata Mater, Danu, Artemis, Ceres, Lug... ...uhtli, Consus, Thor, Vulcan, Thoth, Loki, Vertumnus, E... ...r energies, happiness, transformation. Brown: Earth energies... ...llumination, success, divine power, harvest Green: Abundance... ...vegetation Herb Blackberry: Protection, binding, defense, cle... healing, abundance, friendship, love Allspice: Money, wealth... ...agickal power Basil: Protection, luck, love, wealth, abundance... Solar energies, healing, protection, friendship, peace, cooperat...

*I*N THIS CHAPTER you'll find a collection of meditations, prayers, and invocations designed especially for Lughnasadh. Incorporate them into rituals and spellwork, or simply use them on their own as a way to connect and tune in to the energies of this blessed season.

For many Pagans, prayer is much more than a humble plea for assistance. The act of directly communicating with higher powers and beseeching their aid can be a very hands-on and cooperative experience, a meshing of magickal thought and spiritual concentration for the purpose of forging a connection between one's needs and the ability to satisfy those needs. Pagan prayers are different from the prayers of many other religions, in that Pagan prayers often make use of magickal techniques in order to better convey desires and more effectively carry out intentions. While deities are generally respected as sources of great power, the use of flattery, bribery, and even threats to obtain the help of the gods is not uncommon in Pagan prayer, and rhythm, repetition, visualization, and other magickal techniques might also be incorporated.

Honesty is important in prayer. We all have our own unique conceptions of the Divine, and your prayers will be most effective when aligned to suit your personal understanding of the powers to whom you pray. If it doesn't feel right to you to address a god in a certain way, don't do it! Keep your prayers natural and honest, congruent with your own personal belief system, needs, and desires.

Also keep in mind that a prayer is not an end-all; to many modern Pagans, a prayer is an extra boost, an additional reinforcement, but it is by no means all that needs to be done. Personal actions to back up the prayer are often considered essential in gaining the favor of the forces whose help has been elicited. When we pray, we recognize the god within ourselves as well; as we ask for outside assistance, we also activate our own inner divine potential.

You'll also find in this chapter some suggestions for meditations to try this Lughnasadh. Meditation is the act of spending time in a state of mental stillness or directed focus for the purpose of achieving spiritual aims or simply to induce relaxation. Meditation can take many forms, from aiming for a state of absolute mental stillness to directing focus on a single point such as the movement of one's own breath, or a chanted mantra. Meditation can take the form of directed daydreaming, a time when imagination and intuition join forces to achieve a magickal mental and spiritual state in which astral thoughts can manifest themselves in reality, the physical plane.

You'll also find several invocation in this chapter. Invocation is a magickal process in which a spirit or god is actually called into the physical form of a person or object. The person or object becomes the godform or spirit invoked therein, an open channel through which the summoned spirit can come in and interact with the mundane physical world.

Whether you're invoking a spirit, meditating, or praying, it's helpful to take a moment beforehand to empty your mind of thoughts related to your own personal life or identity. Let go of ego, and try as best you can to open up, becoming an empty vessel into which spirit and spiritual knowledge can pour. Take some deep breaths before you get started, and trust your own inner wisdom to guide you.

Feel free to adapt, expand, and elaborate any of the prayers, invocations, and meditations below as you wish.

Invocation of Lugh

Great Lugh, you whose mother is Ethniu (pronounced EN-yew),
you who are the foster son of Tailtiu (pronounced TAL-chi-uh), *I call on you!*
Great Lugh, you whose father is Cian (pronounced KEEN),
take notice!

Hear my words, great Lugh; hear my plea, great god of skill
  and war!
You who bears the great sword, I ask you to enter me now!
Great Lugh, you who are skilled in all the arts of man,
  come into me now!
Great Lugh, the fierce striker!
Great Lugh, you whose arm is long and reach is strong,
  I call on you to enter me now!
Bright one with the strong hand, enter into me now!
Liberator of the Tuatha Dé Danann! Protector of the earth!
  Great Lugh, come into me!
Join your skill with my own; let these arms wield your mighty spear!
Great Lugh, come into me!
This body is yours. This vessel is yours to fill. This breath,
  this blood, these bones are your own!
Take possession of me, great Lugh!
Great Lugh, take possession, come into me now!

Prayer to Lugh for Strength and Skill

Lord Lugh, great king!
You who are mighty!
You who are great!
Possessor of skill beyond measure!
Possessor of strength beyond compare!

I ask you, Lord Lugh, to help one of your dedicated warriors.

Please help me, Lugh, to increase my strength and skill!

*My victories are yours, Lord Lugh! My accomplishments are yours,
    Lord Lugh!*

*My trophies and treasures won through strength and skill are your
    own, Lord Lugh!*

Bind your strength to my own, Lord Lugh!

Fill my mind and hands with your skill, Lord Lugh!

*If I fail, may my failure be your own! If I'm weak, let my weakness
    be your own!*

Hear me now, Lord Lugh, and look after your own!

Fill me with strength and with skill!

Bind your power, Lord Lugh, to my own!

The victories will be yours.

*The accomplishments will be yours—the glory, the trophies,
    the treasures, your own!*

I give my all to you, Lord Lugh, so that together we might prevail!

Let your warrior prevail, Lord Lugh!

Let there be no room for failure!

Leave me no place to back down!

*Take my hands in your own, Lord Lugh; give me strength and skill
    to serve you well!*

Prayer to Lugh for Protection of Land

Lugh, foster son of Tailtiu, stepchild of she who is the mother of the
  plowed fields,

I call on you to listen to me now, Lugh!

Your mother needs you!

Your bride, the earth, awaits you!

You are the king of this land; protect your sovereign right!

King Lugh, I ask you to protect this ground!

Protect this land!

Protect this earth on which we stand!

Strike down the storms with your spear, Lugh!

Fight off the pests with your sword of power!

Stave off all threats to this land, this earth!

Protect this land with your mighty power!

Protect this land, your own holy kingdom!

Place your strength and power and protection right here!

Strength! Power! Protection!

Lugh's mighty spear and sword are poised above!

No one can harm here!

No storms can come here!

Soft rains will fall here!

Sunbeams will shine here!

If great Lugh decrees it, then so will it be!

Protect this place, Lugh! So will it be!

Invocation of Danu

Dear Danu, great goddess!
Mother of the Tuatha!
Great Lady of the water!
Great Ruler of the land!
Dear Danu, great goddess,
I invoke thee!
Fill me with your strength!
Fill me with your grace!
Fill me with your power!
May your eyes look through my face!
Great Danu,
Mother of the River!
Mother of the Land!
Mother of the People!
Come into my hands!
Danu, I invoke thee!
Come to me now!
Great mother, great Danu, come into me now!

Prayer to Danu for Abundance

Dear Danu, my mother, please hear me!

Great goddess of the earth!

Great lady of the water!

Great mother of the growing green!

Dear Danu, my mother, I pray to you!

Like the earth, may my life be filled with abundance!

May the fields overflow with ripe vegetables!

May my purse overflow with wealth!

May the trees be laden with ripened fruits!

May my pockets be heavy with riches!

Great Danu, gracious mother, bless me as you bless the earth!

Bring abundance to the land!

Bring abundance to my hand!

Bring abundance to the land!

Bring abundance to my hand!

Great Danu, gracious Danu, to you I pray with all my heart!

Bring abundance to the earth!

Bring abundance to my heart!

Prayer to Danu for Victory

Mother Danu, great Goddess!

Great Queen of the earth and waters!

I am one of your own, great Danu!

Please hear me, great Goddess!

Guide me to victory!

Make me brave and strong and fierce like one of your own!

I am one of your own, great Danu!

Guide me to victory like one of your own!

I break through my obstacles!

I stomp on my challengers!

I crush defeat like a tiny insect!

Victory is mine and yours, great Danu!

Guide me, great Goddess, to serve you well!

With you, I will conquer!

For you, I will win!

The glory of victory is yours alone, great Danu!

Make me fierce!

Make me brave!

Let us conquer!

Let us win!

As great Danu wills it,

so will we win!

Gratitude Meditation

As the fields come to fruition and offer us their bountiful harvest, Lughnasadh is a fitting time for a gratitude meditation. Take this opportunity to reflect on all the blessings in your life. Find a quiet place to do this meditation, preferably somewhere outdoors. Close your eyes and let your thoughts settle. Observe your thoughts and emotions, letting them flow through you freely. It may take some time before your mind becomes clear, so be patient and don't fight your mind. Just let it happen, and try not to grasp on to any particular thought or emotion that comes through you. Once you feel like your mind is as clear and settled as it's likely to get, begin the meditation.

Imagine yourself surrounded by a field of ripened fruits, vegetables, or grains. How do you feel surrounded by this bounty? Look to the edges of the field. Do you see or sense any images of other things in your life for which you're grateful? Are there friends? Family? Fortunate circumstances that have occurred recently?

Do you have any messages to convey to this "field of dreams"? Express your feelings of gratitude by projecting your thoughts and emotions outward into the visualized space around you. You might even imagine yourself giving gifts to each person or circumstance occurring in your vision. When you've finished, open your eyes, take some slow, deep breaths, and reenter a state of normal wakeful consciousness. Spend some time reflecting on your experience. You might want to write about what happened or perhaps paint a picture of your visions and emotions.

Meditation on Reaping and Sowing

For those of us who aren't gardeners or farmers, relating our own lives to the ideas of reaping and sowing can be helpful in connecting us with the energies of the Lughnasadh season. Try this simple meditation. Sit comfortably, allow your thoughts to drift and settle, then begin.

Envision yourself in an empty field. The ground has not yet been tilled. Look around. Do you see any gardening tools you could use to till the soil? Imagine yourself readying the field for planting, and think about the preparations and efforts and planning you've put toward achieving your own personal dreams and life goals. Now look at your body. Are you carrying any seeds, perhaps in your pockets or in a bag strapped to your back or slung at your side? Take the seeds in your hand, and examine them. What dreams and goals do these seeds represent? Are you hopeful or doubtful that they will grow to full fruition?

Envision the sunlight streaming down on the seeds in your hand, filling them with a magickal, fertile energy that will ensure their successful growth. Now imagine yourself planting your super-charged dream seeds, one by one, carefully patting down the soft earth around each one. Envision yourself pouring water on the seeds, and see them sprouting and growing right before your eyes. What will these little sprouts grow into? Imagine your dream plants growing to full maturity, and envision the ripened "fruit" of your creation. Visualize all your dreams and goals having come true, and see yourself experiencing the joy and satisfaction of that future moment of certainty when you'll know your harvest has been successfully reaped. Envision yourself walking away from the field, smiling and confident. Come back to your everyday consciousness, then take at least one solid, physical action toward achieving your goals.

Prayer for the Consecration of Bread

Great spirit of the harvest, great mother of the grain!
This bread is your body; come into it!
Great goddess of abundance! Great goddess of the fruitful fields!
This bread is your body; come into it!
Great goddess of the harvest! Great mother of the grain!
Fill this bread with your spirit!
Fill our bodies with your spirit!
Let us taste the flesh of living spirit!
Bless this bread and make it your body!
Your holy body will be as our bread!
This bread is the flesh of your living spirit,
and we welcome your body to be in our own!

Prayer to Ops for Fertility of Mind, Body, and Spirit

Great Ops, Opis, lady of the earth, the fields, the growing things!

Lady of fertility and plenty!

Great goddess of the prolific bounty!

Great goddess of the fruits and grains!

Hear my plea, great lady!

Make me fertile like the fields!

Prolific like the fruit trees!

Let me manifest my wishes as you manifest the fruits and grains!

Touch me, Ops, and make me fertile!

Touch me, Ops, and help me grow!

Make me as a cultivated field, ready for the seed!

Fertile and thriving you make me!

Prolific and bountiful like the fields and the trees!

Touch me, great Ops, and grant me your blessing!

Make me fertile and thriving!

Allow me to grow!

If great Ops decrees it, then it will be so!

Prayer to the Nymphs for the Protection of Trees

Friends of Artemis, protectors of the trees!

Defenders of the grove! Warrior maidens of the forest!

Protectors of the mountain heights!

Hear me now!

Great protectors of the mighty oak!

Great warriors of the ash!

Caretakers of the apple!

Defenders of the walnut!

Protectors of the mulberry!

Warriors of the laurel!

Caretakers of the elm!

Defenders of the mountains!

Protectors of the sacred groves!

Warriors of the vales!

Caretakers of the glens!

Hear me now, and protect your kin!

Rise up, mighty maidens, and protect your kin!

Protect the trees all over the land!

Let no harm come from the hand of man!

All your strength and might and power,

to the trees, to thrive and flower!

Warriors, defenders, protectors of trees! Hear me!

You must rise up and protect your own!

Extend your reach and protect your own!

Both near and far, they are your own!
Your sacred kin are in great need,
and bound to serve, you are decreed!
Rise up, great nymphs from far and near!
Protect the trees that you hold dear!
Not a saw shall cut the bark!
Not a storm shall freeze the crown!
Not an ax shall chop it down!
Forevermore, the trees are sound!

RITUALS
OF
CELEBRATION

...ion, introspection, discernment, sacrifice, excellent time for mag...

...y, abundance, strength, growth, protection, honoring ancestors,

...sformation, or communications with the dead; sacred wells, be...

...s for magick, astronomical midpoint between the Summer So...

...at 15 degrees Leo in the Northern Hemisphere, Sun at

...uarius in the Southern Hemisphere, Mother Goddess, Earth

Goddess, water nymphs, tree nymphs, the spirit of the land,

...Earth God, Solar God, the warrior, the protector, the sa...

...he dying god, the spirit of vegetation, the newly crowned king

...Dryads, Demeter, Kore, Iwannotar, Nemesis, Ops, No...

...Juturna, Stata Mater, Danu, Artemis, Osiris, Zu...

...cihtli, Consus, Thor, Vulcan, Thoth, Loabi, Vertumnus, ...

...r energies, happiness, transformation. Brown: Earth energies,

...llumination, success, divine power, harvest. Green: Abundance

...vegetation. Herb Blackberry: Protection, binding, defense, ...

...healing, abundance, friendship, love. Allspice: Money, wealt...

...magickal power. Basil: Protection, luck, love, wealth, abundanc...

...Solar energies, healing, protection, friendship, peace, keep ...

$\mathcal{L}$UGHNASADH IS A season of harvest, a season of creation and culmination, a season of union and of sacrifice. It's a great time for rituals intended to express gratitude for the bounties of life and to bolster protection for the earth and its plants. It's also a great time to get in sync with the energies of Mother Earth and connect with the spirit of vegetation. In this chapter you'll find several rituals especially designed to help you make the most of this season's magick and mystery.

Rituals are different from spells, although spells might be performed within the course of a ritual. Rituals are usually (but not necessarily) more in-depth and more complex than spells, and their effects are typically longer-lasting. In a ritual there is often direct communication and contact with higher spiritual entities, whereas this may or may not be the case with a spell. There is spiritual purpose in the art of ritual, a value placed on the experience alone, independent from the magickal outcome. A spell may or may not have a spiritual purpose, whereas a ritual always does.

Below you'll find a ritual to do with a larger group, a ritual for solitary practice, a ritual to do with a partner, and a super-quick mini-ritual to do when you only have a few moments to spare. Feel free to personalize these rituals with your own adjustments and additions.

Group Ritual to Honor the Corn

You'll have an easier time and a lot more fun if you do this ritual with a group, but it's also effective as a solitary ritual or two-person ritual. This ritual honors the spirit of the vegetation that has given its life and energy for the sake of the harvest.

Purpose:

The purpose of this ritual is to show respect to the spirit of the vegetation and to express gratitude for the harvest, allowing ritualists to more deeply connect to these energies and tune in to the seasonal flow.

Setting:

Late afternoon approaching evening, outdoors in your own yard or garden, or near a waterside, field, hilltop, or other peaceful area

Supplies:

large supply of corn husks, sticks, sheaves of wheat

Heavy string or twine

Heavy-duty scissors

Food and/or beverage for offerings (you might choose fruit, bread, ale, mead, wine, water, etc.)

Simple snack or meal for ritualists to share

Chair

Paint (optional)

Cup of water (optional)

Hand drum (optional)

Small pillow

Flowers or wreaths

Pre-Ritual Preparations:

To prepare for this ritual, spend some time thinking about this first major harvest of the summer, both the literal harvest of growing plants, and the metaphorical harvest of all the good things your own work and efforts have brought to you. Think about the sacrifice required for the bounty, and get in touch with your honest, genuine feelings regarding this sacrifice, be they feelings of gratitude, sorrow, or fear. You'll also need to place a chair (perhaps adding to it a small pillow, if you like) within the ritual space.

The Ritual:

First, you'll need to create an effigy, or symbolic representation, of the spirit of vegetation. You'll need a good supply of corn husks, sticks, sheaves of wheat, or other plant matter. Even if you've gathered these materials beforehand, look around your chosen ritual site and see if there is anything else you might want to add. You'll also need on hand some sturdy string and a pair of scissors.

Have everyone work together to build the effigy. Choose a stick and surround it with a thick bundle of plant matter, securing it onto the stick by tying it around with pieces of string. You now have the torso or body of your harvest god. Tie on additional sticks and plant matter to create the arms, legs, and head. Use the corn husks to finish the creation, smoothing them flat and covering the various parts to give the doll more bulk and a more rounded-out appearance. Create hair with the wheat, and add a face by painting on a corn husk and attaching it to the head with string.

You're now ready to begin the ritual. You might start by casting a circle. Casting a circle is a ritual technique that encloses a specified space (such as your magickal work space) within an orb-shaped field of positive energy. The circle serves to keep unwanted energies out while keeping desired energies in. When a circle is cast, the energies necessary for the magickal working will more easily "stay put" while being magnified, reprogrammed, and redirected through the actions of the ritualists.

Whether or not you make circle casting a part of the magickal process is up to you, and how you do it if you *do* choose to do so is up to you, also. You might project a feeling of love and light out of your eyes, hands, or through the tip of your wand, sending this feeling into the ritual space and surrounding the area in an orb of sacred light. You might place a ring of protective stones around the space. You might simply visualize a circle of positive, protective power. There are many methods of circle casting, and if you experiment, you'll probably find a technique that suits you. Since this is a Lughnasadh ritual, you might consider giving the circle-casting operation a harvest-themed twist, by casting the circle using a cup of water to symbolize life and fertility, and a sprig of dried wheat to symbolize sacrifice and the bounty of the first harvest.

Have the group stand in a circle, and choose a leader to perform the primary duties of the circle-casting, though everyone in the group can and should be a part of the process. The leader begins by dipping the wheat in the water and then holding this outward, pointed away from the body as if it were a magick wand. The leader then focuses their thoughts on the energy still residing in the wheat, sensing also the life-force flowing through the water that covers it. As the energies of the wheat and the water mingle together, the leader sends through the shaft of the wheat the power of his or her own loving energy, conjuring up a feeling of joy, love, and brightness and projecting this feeling throughout their body, down their arm, through the wheat, and out into the ritual space. The leader might envision this force pushing out any negative energies lingering in the circle, filling the entirety of the space with the loving power emanating from the tip of the wheat. The other ritualists can join in and help, holding their palms open and out and directing their own loving energy out through their palms and into the circle. Finally, the leader should seal off the circle, focusing will and intention on containing the energy within the circle and keeping out any external energies unless they're specifically invited into the magickal space.

Now it's time to send out such invitations, welcoming any deities or powers you wish to work with and inviting them to enter the circle for the course of the rite. Save inviting the spirit of vegetation for last, as you'll be invoking this entity directly into the effigy you made prior to the ritual. When you're ready, place the effigy on the altar if you're using one, or else lay it down directly on the ground in the middle of the ritual space.

Have everyone place their hands upon the effigy. Turn thoughts, emotions, and visualizations towards the land, the vegetation, the harvest. With all hands on the effigy, chant:

Spirit of the harvest, spirit of the land,
Come into your body; come in through our hands!

Repeat this chant until there becomes an obvious difference in the way the effigy feels; it may become hot to the touch, or particularly vibrant, or perhaps it will begin to pulse, almost as if it were breathing. You might sense a presence, a powerful spirit among you that wasn't there before. However it manifests, if the invocation is successful, it should become fairly clear at some point that the spirit of the vegetation has indeed taken up temporary residence within the effigy. Once this occurs, the ritual leader should place one of their hands on the head of the effigy and the other one on the chest of the effigy, roughly where the heart would be. The other ritualists should begin walking around the circle clockwise to build up the energy within the space in order to help solidify and seal the invocation. Drumming at a steady heartbeat rhythm at this stage can aid in the process. With hands still placed on the effigy, the ritual leader chants in a rising crescendo:

The spirit resides within this, and within this the spirit is sewn!

The chant is repeated until the ritual leader feels that the invocation is complete, the effigy now animated with the living spirit of vegetation.

At this point, the group should show the spirit of vegetation a good time in whatever ways seem suitable. First, if your effigy has been lying on the ground, give it a nicer place to rest, placing it on the chair and providing it with a soft pillow for greater comfort and luxury. You might want to treat your honored guest to some libations also, pouring ale, water, or other beverage on its mouth. If you have drums, play some lively music and dance for a while. You might even take turns dancing with the spirit of vegetation itself. Express your gratitude to the spirit of vegetation, offering thanks for the current harvest and acknowledging the continued work the spirit must do throughout the rest of the growing season. Let the party wane naturally, slowing the drums to a more mellow pace as everyone begins to run out of steam. Place any flowers or wreaths upon the effigy, and leave it in place or give it a prominent space in the garden until the second or third harvest, when it can be incorporated into further rituals according to personal choice and traditions.

Solitary Ritual–Day in the Life of the Goddess

In Celtic lore, it was not Lugh but Lugh's divine stepmother, Tailtiu, who was originally honored at Lughnasadh, the Tailteann games being instituted in honor of her labor and sacrifice in preparing the fields of Ireland for agriculture. Lughnasadh is a great time to honor goddess energies in your own life, giving thanks to mother earth and reconnecting to the goddess qualities of beauty, compassion, inspiration, and tenacity. Here's a ritual to help you do just that. Though designed especially for solitary practice, it can be performed by couples and groups, as well.

As a day-long ritual, this ceremony is a little different from the typical sabbat rite. You'll begin this ritual first thing in the morning.

Purpose:
This ritual will help you get in touch with goddess energies and get in sync with the season's power flow.

Setting:
Indoors or outdoors, beginning first thing in the morning and continuing until sunset

Supplies:
One small apple
Athame or other small blade

Pre-Ritual Preparations:
Take a purifying ritual bath or shower before you begin the ritual, envisioning any negative or stale energies flowing out of your body and into the water, leaving you cleansed, refreshed,

and balanced. If you like, dress in a manner that you feel will help you to tune in to the energies of the goddess; you might choose fabrics of white, red, black, or silver, or you might wear jewelry featuring goddess symbols such as moons or pears.

The Ritual:

Choose a small apple (the smaller the better, as you'll be carrying this with you all day). Hold the apple in your hand and ask goddess energies to enter into the fruit and spend the day with you. Think of this goddess energy in whatever way you personally conceive it; you might call on a specific goddess by name, or simply think about the characteristics you associate with femininity, mothering, and female strength and power.

Now it's time to think about how you and the goddess might spend the day. You might consider engaging in several different activities to get in touch with various goddess energies. For instance, you might choose an activity to coincide with the idea of Beauty, an activity to coincide with the idea of Compassion, an activity to coincide with the idea of Tenacity, and an activity to coincide with the idea of Inspiration. Below, you'll find suggested activities for connecting to each of these goddess energies, but by no means should you feel limited or restricted by this. You can choose additional qualities or entirely different qualities to focus on, and you can pick whatever activities seem the most appealing to you. What you'll find below are suggestions to help you envision how your own creative ritual might play out. Whatever activities you choose to do for the ritual, place the apple in a pocket, purse, bag, or backpack before you get started, and keep the fruit with you throughout the course of the day's adventures.

If beauty is one of the goddess qualities you wish to connect to, consider starting the day by taking a little extra care with your appearance. Wear something that makes you feel attractive, and remember that today, the goddess is wearing these clothes, too. Think of the most appealing and beautiful people you can imagine, and envision this beauty as a radiant, golden light. Imagine this light coming into you, entering your body through your chest then flowing upwards and shining back out through your now magickally enhanced, beautiful face. Feel attractive, and walk like you feel you're attractive.

Not that confident? Play make-believe if you have to; pretend you are a super great actor who is *acting* like the most beautiful person on earth, and adjust your posture, stride, and facial expressions to match accordingly. Go for a walk somewhere where you're likely to encounter other people. Envision your beauty radiating outward to affect everyone you pass by or meet, enchanting their hearts, minds, and bodies with a feeling of confidence, excitement, and joy. You might also connect with the idea of beauty by taking time to enjoy the beauty of Nature; consider a stroll through the garden or a walk along the riverfront as you strive to notice as much beauty in the outside world and its creatures as possible.

Next, you might decide to focus on the goddess quality of Compassion. Try to invoke this quality as much as possible, and choose something nice to do for someone. You might donate food or clothing to the needy, or simply listen to someone lonely or troubled who needs someone caring to talk to. Just make sure whatever you choose to do is truly from the heart; showy acts of charity are shallow and won't produce the desired effects for this ritual.

For the next stage of the ritual, you might choose to connect with the goddess quality of Inspiration. To be inspiring, you must first be inspired, so go to a place you find special, somewhere that invigorates your mind and energizes your spirit. This might be a park, an art museum, a playground, a beach, a friend's house, or even a rock concert—the point is to do something that *you* like, something that leaves you feeling refreshed and full of fresh creative energy. Once you're in the zone, you might spread some of that good feeling around. Be a muse: you might say something inspiring to a perfect stranger, make some cool chalk art in the park and leave the chalk there so others can make art, too, go to a dance club and encourage the shy folks to get up and dance, give someone a musical instruments or art supplies, or any number of equally inspiring acts. Focus on encouraging creativity and imagination to flow through everyone you encounter, and you won't go wrong.

Finally, you might focus on the goddess energy of Tenacity. For this, you'll need to find some real work to do, something that will require great effort, stamina, and determination in order to see it through. You might connect with goddess energies further by choosing an activity that will be a true labor of love, done for the benefit of someone or something other than yourself. Love and compassion are often tenacity's fuel, after all. If you're physically able, you might clean up a local park, or spend some time picking up trash in a polluted neighborhood. As another option, you might volunteer some time to help a neighbor or friend in need—just ask around, and you'll most likely find someone willing to gratefully accept your offer.

You may feel that a more personal challenge will better show you the ins and outs of what being tenacious is all about. If that's the case, you might use breaking a bad habit or avoiding an unhealthy but favored snack as a way to boost your tenacity and get in touch with this strong and determined aspect of goddess energies. This part of the ritual can potentially last for as long as you like and are able to endure, and the length will depend a great deal on the activity you've selected. If you've chosen something like avoiding cigarettes, consider *keeping on* avoiding them even after the ritual is complete. If you've decided to do some physical exercise, don't wear yourself past your limits. Whatever you choose, make sure it's challenging, and most importantly, always keep in mind your overall health and welfare.

By the time evening rolls around, you and your goddess apple will have had a long day. Take the apple out and hold it in your hand as you sit back and relax somewhere comfortable. This might be your favorite recliner, a bench at a local park, or a mat in front of your altar. Rest a little with the apple in your hand, breathing slowly and reflecting on all the day's activities that you and the goddess apple shared. Once you've spent some time reflecting and you've got your energy reserves back up, it's time to move on to the final stage of the ritual.

Place the apple on your altar or in the center of your ritual space. If you like, cast a magick circle around the area. The energies of the goddess are already there in the apple, but if there are any other deities or energies you wish to join in the ritual, invite them now. Formally welcome any spirits that enter the ritual space, then direct attention to the apple on the altar. Place your hands on the apple and address the goddess therein with this verse or with words of your own:

Great Lady, Great Goddess, Great Mother of the Earth!
Great Lady of Beauty!
Great Goddess of Compassion!

Tenacious Mother and Source of Inspiration!
Today I walked with you, and today you walked with me.
Thank you, Gracious Goddess, for all the things you helped me see!

Spend some time reflecting on the thoughts and emotions lingering within you following the day's events. Did you learn anything from your experiences? Do you feel more connected to the divine feminine, to the earth, or to the earth's creatures? Did you gain new insights into the goddess energies you invoked? Did you engage in any activities today or practice any goddess qualities that you wish to develop into a regular habit even after the ritual is complete? Think about what you did and what you learned, and thank the goddess for the experience.

Now, ask the goddess if she has any new insights to share. Using a ritual athame or other blade, cut the apple in half horizontally, so that you can see a cross-section of the core. Notice how the apple seeds are arranged in a star formation, and gaze at this spot. Let your eyes become relaxed, and blink normally as you forget about what you're seeing in front of you and begin instead to gain awareness of what you're seeing within you. As your thoughts wander, notice the images emanating from your mind's eye. Pay attention to the visions that come to you; trust what you sense and try to see more details in the images you're seeing within your head. When you've finished and your mind comes back to more "normal" ritual consciousness, reflect on the visions received, maybe even writing a few notes about it if it suits you to do so.

Express thanks a final time, dismiss the energies present, cut the circle if you cast one, and eat the fruit altar-side to complete the ritual. Leave any unfinished apple scraps outside so that animals can enjoy them.

Couple's Ritual—Wedding Feast

Many Neopagans today think of Lughnasadh as "Lugh's Wedding Feast," a celebration of the marriage of the god Lugh (widely conceived in modern times as a solar deity) to the goddess of earth, an idea often understood symbolically and metaphorically as the joining of the sun to the land. Why not celebrate Lughnasadh with a wedding feast ritual of your own? Here's an idea for a wedding feast ritual intended to help gain protection for the earth and its vegetation.

This is a physically intimate ritual designed for couples, but it can also be enacted by larger groups of multiple ritualists.

Purpose:

The purpose of this ritual is to gain magickal protection for the earth, its crops, and its wild vegetation. It will also help ritualists experience some of the deeper mysteries of Lughnasadh.

Setting:

Day or night, somewhere safe, private, and comfortable, preferably outdoors

Supplies:

dirt and/or plants
goblet
red wine or water
soft pillows (optional)
blankets (optional)
music (optional)
two chairs (optional)

Pre-Ritual Preparations:

Spend some time thinking about the inner weaving of nature's various forces. How do the earth, sun, winds, and rains work together to make the crops grow? Can plants grow without the earth? Can plants grow without the sun? The sun needs the earth as a medium through which to create, and the earth needs the sun to activate its inner potentials of creation. Think about the interdependence and interconnectedness of the earth and the sun, the earth and its many plants and creatures and other life forms. You'll also want to spend some time relaxing before the ritual, perhaps with a slow stroll out in nature, by listening to your favorite music, by taking a calming ritual bath, or with anything else that suits you. You want to feel comfortable, free from worry, and open to magickal experience; accomplish this with whatever means you find work best.

The Ritual:

Begin by selecting a person or persons to represent the land, the crops, the earth, and choose the person or persons who will be taking on the role of Lugh, who might be seen as a representation of the sky or sun. If the ritual is being performed by more than two people, choose someone to act as the "leader" of each group, one to represent the land faction, and one to represent the sky/solar faction. You can go skyclad (nude) for this ritual (as you're likely to end up that way, anyway), or you might decide to don ritual garb to start, opting for earthy tones like browns, greens, blues, golds, or whites.

To begin, prepare the ritual space. You'll want it to be comfortable and inviting. Place soft pillows and blankets in the space, or find a soft patch of grass or a comfy pile of leaves to serve as your ritual area. Light an incense that's associated with love, divinity, and passion, such as jasmine or myrrh. You might want to play some music to help set the mood for magick. Cast a circle around the space if desired, and get ready to get started.

The person representing the land should lie down in the middle of the ritual space, palms flat on the ground and the body ready to become a reciprocal of the spirit of the earth. Feel the energy of the earth coming into your body, connecting fully with your own energies. Envision the meridian of energy that stretches from the top of your head all the way down to your feet, and imagine that this energetic current is bound to the energies emanating up from the earth. Now think of farmland, crops, soil, wild plants springing up from the earth, and conjure in the heart a motherly feeling of strength and nurturing. This feeling is then projected outward into the ritual area, leaving behind an open space in the heart— sort of a doorway of light— through which the Goddess will enter. Either mentally or out loud, the person representing land might say:

Great Mother of the Earth, Great Mother of the land,
Great Mother of the crops and wild plants and trees!
Come into me now!
I am your vessel; come into me now!
Great Goddess! Great Mother! You are life! You are land!
Come into me now, Great Goddess! Come into me now, the land!
Great Goddess! Great Mother!
Great Goddess of the crops and wild plants and trees!
Come into me now, my Mother! Enter into me; I am the land!

The other ritualist or ritualists can help facilitate the invocation by rubbing dirt or plants on the body of the person being filled with this holy spirit. When the invocation succeeds and the ritualist has been transformed temporarily into the Earth Goddess, embodiment of the land and the crops and the wild growing things, they can continue to rest comfortably, take a seat, or choose to stand—the important thing is to "stay in the zone" and don't slip back into usual-self consciousness until the ritual is complete. For this reason, it might be a good idea to have a couple of special chairs already placed in the ritual area, to serve as thrones for the guests of honor (Land and Sky) once these spirits are invoked into the bodies of the ritualists.

Next, the person representing the sun and sky takes center stage. Standing with open body posture, arms raised in a V above the head and feet shoulder-width apart, the person invoking the sky might focus their attentions above, feeling the power of the atmosphere, the power of the air, the wind, the sun. It can help to disengage the root chakra, the energy center connecting your feet to the earth below. Envision the energy in this area as a glowing orb of light, then consciously direct that orb of light to rise through your body, upwards until it reaches the top of your head, the location of the crown chakra which connects your body's energy with the energy of the skies and higher realms. As the energy moves through you, you will feel it as it hits each major chakra along the way; you might sense the energy spinning, gaining power as it rotates and rises higher. Once the energy has moved to the crown chakra, envision this energy as a cord stretching upwards out of the top of your head to connect with the sun and sky. Say to yourself or state out loud:

Great Father of the Sky, Great God of the Sun,
Great Protector of the Goddess Mother Earth!
Come into me now!
I am your vessel; come into me now!
Dear Lord! Dear Father! You are the warrior on whom we depend!
Come into me now, Great God!
Come into me now, Great Father of the Sky, Great God of the Sun!
Great God! Great Father! Great Protector
of the Goddess Mother Earth!
Come into me now, my Father!
Enter into me; I am the sky!
Enter into me; I am the sun!
Enter into me, great god of the sky!
Enter into me and make us one!

The other ritualist or ritualists can help at this stage by envisioning white, fluffy clouds or gently swirling winds surrounding the person invoking the sky. Once the invocation is successful, the Sky takes their place by their partner, the Land.

Land and Sky lock eyes, and Land offers Sky a drink of red wine or water from a goblet. Land says, "Welcome, Sky." Sky drinks the liquid and hands the cup back to Land, saying, "Thank you, Land, and welcome."

Land then says, "Great Sky, your protection is needed to safeguard my fruits and my flowers. Taste my essence, and join your strength with my own!"

Land and Sky share a kiss, then Sky embraces Land and says, "Great Land, I am bound to you forever! Through you only may I share my strength, my power, and to you I offer my essence to use as you will!"

The two continue to embrace, letting the embrace become caresses, and allowing kisses and more heavy touching to flow naturally if both partners are so inclined. If there are other people participating in the ritual and everyone feels comfortable, you might enjoy a group cuddle at this point. Take the touching as far as everyone desires and not beyond anyone's comfort zone. Let the stimulation build as much as you like, as this energy magnifies the magickal power that's already present and also helps to forge the bond between Sky and Land. Once you're ready for this stage of the ritual to come to an end, raise the sexual energy to a height once more as Sky and Land embrace and press their bodies tightly together. Say, "Land is joined to Sky, and Sky is joined to Land. We have forged a pact of love and power; our oath will not be broken!"

Next, Land and Sky walk together hand in hand in a circle around the ritual space, chanting:

Protected are the crops!
Protected is the land!
Protected are the trees, the roots, the leaves!
Protected are the wild growing things!
Protected are the tender shoots!
Protected are the blossoming fruits!
Protected are the ripening gourds, protected are the greens!
Protected is the bountiful harvest!
Protected is the Mother of Earth!
Protected are the children of the sky and of the land!
As we will it, then so will it be!
A pact is forged between Land, Sky, and We!

The ritual is now complete. Dismiss the spirits of the Sky and Land and any other powers you invited to join you for this magickal ceremony.

Quick Mini Ritual—Bread and Blessings

Like any sabbat, Lughnasadh can be a very busy time, what with all the planning and preparation and cooking and such that's often involved. Here's a quick and easy Lughnasadh ritual you can do in just a couple of minutes to get you re-centered and re-focused on the deeper meanings of this special day whenever stress threatens to make your holiday feel hectic.

Purpose:
The purpose of this ritual is to express gratitude for your blessings and to attract even greater good fortune, leaving you feeling centered, focused, relaxed, and ready to enjoy a wonderful sabbat.

Setting:
Outdoors, anytime day or night

Supplies:
piece of bread
glass of water
compass (optional)

Pre-Ritual Preparations:
Shake your body vigorously, moving your arms and legs, head and neck. This will help release any lingering stress and get you ready to enter a magickal mindset. You'll also want to determine the cardinal directions, using a compass if necessary to find north, south, east, and west.

The Ritual:

Carry the piece of bread and glass of water outside, and stand tall, holding these objects in your hands. Think of how it feels to be hungry and thirsty, and how that piece of bread and glass of water can mean so much when we are in a place of need. Think of the blessings in your life—food, water, friends and family, the sunshine, and the earth beneath your feet. Break the bread into four pieces, and moving clockwise, place a piece in each of the four directions, north, east, south, and west.

Each cardinal point corresponds to one of the four elements—north with earth, east with air, south with fire, and west with water. As you place the bread in the northern quadrant, express your thanks for the good things in life you associate with the earth element—material wealth, security, stability, manifestation, the food, the harvest, the soil, the crops, and the wild vegetation. As you place the bread in the eastern quadrant, express your gratitude for any blessings you associate with the air element—change, movement, circulation, breath, the atmosphere, fluidity, thought, intelligence, and conscious action. As you place the bread in the southern quadrant, express thanks for any good fortune you've had in areas of your life you might associate with the fire element—transformation, light, warmth, the sun, illumination, energy, and cleansing destruction. As you place the bread in the western quadrant, express your thanks for the blessings you associate with the water element—love, emotion, life, blood, the currents of creativity and creation. To conclude the ritual, turn clockwise around the circle once more, this time slowly pouring out a ring of water from the glass as you rotate. While making this final rotation, say out loud or to yourself:

"I give my thanks to the powers that be!
To these powers, connect
the powers of me!
This, we will it, and so it will be!"

Repeat the chant for as long as it takes you to make the full rotation around the circle. Reserve a final sip of water for yourself, and drink it to conclude the ritual.

CORRESPONDENCES
FOR
LUGHNASADH

...tion, introspection, discernment, sacrifice, excellent time for ma...
...ity, abundance, strength, growth, protection, honoring ancestor...
...nsformation, or communicating with the dead, sacred wells, ...
...ls for magick, astronomical midpoint between the Summer ...
...n at 15 degrees Leo in the Northern Hemisphere, Sun a...
...quarius in the Southern Hemisphere, Mother Goddess, Ea...
... Goddess, water nymphs, tree nymphs, the spirit of the land ...
...n, Earth God, Solar God, the warrior, the protector, the s...
...the dying god, the spirit of vegetation, the newly crowned kin...
...Dryads, Demeter, Kore, Luannotar, Nemesis, Ops, ...
..., Juturna, Stata Mater, Danu, Artemis, Ceres, L...
...tcuhtli, Consus, Thor, Vulcan, Thoth, Lohi, Vertumnus, ...
...tar energies, happiness, transformation. Brown: Earth energies...
...Illumination, success, divine power, harvest Green: Abundan...
...h, vegetation Herb Blackberry: Protection, binding, defense, a...
... healing, abundance, friendship, love Allspice: Money, mea...
...magickal power Basil: Protection, luck, love, wealth, abundan...
...Solar energies, healing, protection, friendship, peace, inspir...

Spiritual Focus and Keywords

gratitude

abundance

blessings

the necessity and inevitability of both life and death

celebration

harvest

reflection

introspection

discernment

sacrifice

Magickal Focus and Suggested Workings

excellent time for magick focused on prosperity

gratitude

abundance

strength

growth

protection

honoring ancestors
making offerings in exchange for blessings
personal transformation
communicating with the dead

Sacred wells, hilltops, and cemeteries are ideal sites for magickal workings. It's also a great time to collect wild herbs and make new tools for magick.

Astrological timing and associated planets

Astronomical midpoint between the Summer Solstice and Autumn Equinox; Sun at 15 degrees Leo in the Northern Hemisphere, Sun at 15 degrees Aquarius in the Southern Hemisphere. Some Pagans time the sabbat astronomically, while others hold the celebration on August 1, typically beginning at sundown July 31 and ending at the next sundown. Other Pagans celebrate on August 5, which is called "Old Lammas," or "Old Style Lammas." Still others time the sabbat in accordance with cues from Nature, celebrating when the wild berries become ripe, or when the first crops of the harvest reach fruition.

Archetypes

FEMALE

mother goddess

earth goddess

water goddess

water nymphs

tree nymphs

the pregnant mother

the exhausted mother

the selfless mother

the nurturer

the spirit of the land

the established queen

MALE

father god

earth god

solar god

the warrior

the protector

the sacrificial god

the dying god

the spirit of vegetation

the newly crowned king

Deities and Heroes

GODDESSES

Tailtiu (Celtic)

Isis (Egyptian)

Dryads (Greek)

Demeter (Greek)

Kore (Greek)

Luannotar (Finnish)

Nemesis (Greek)

Ops (Roman)

Hathor (Egyptian)

Hecate (Greek)

Diana (Roman)

Pomona (Roman)

Juturna (Roman)

Stata Mater (Roman)

Danu (Celtic)

Artemis (Greek)

GODS

Osiris (Egyptian)

Lugh (Celtic)

Ganesha Chaturthi (Hindu)

Xiuhtecuhtli (Aztec)

Consus (Roman)

Thor (Norse)

Vulcan (Roman)

Thoth (Egyptian)

Loki (Norse)

Vertumnus (Roman)

Apollo (Roman)

Ragbod (Norse)

Colors

Yellow: Solar energies, happiness, transformation

Brown: Earth energies, strength, protection, wealth, animals

Gold: Illumination, success, divine power, harvest

Green: Abundance, prosperity, fertility, growth, wealth, life,
   health, vegetation

Herbs

Blackberry: Protection, binding, defense, abundance, strength,
   passion

Bilberry: Protection, healing, abundance, friendship, love

Allspice: Money, wealth, prosperity, luck, strength, tenacity,
   magickal power

Basil: Protection, luck, love, wealth, abundance, psychic
   insight

Rosemary: Solar energies, healing, protection, friendship,
   peace, cooperation, love, abundance

Garlic: Protection, strength, defense, purification, courage

Bay: Victory, protection, binding, psychic power, prosperity, spirit communication, dream magick

Fennel: Purification, defense, courage, protection, clarity

Trees

Apple: Goddess energies, abundance, love, passion, strength, communicating with the dead, beauty

Hazelnut: Psychic insight, wisdom, clarity, love, creativity, fertility, luck, protection, magickal power

Holly: Protection, defense, binding, strength, tenacity, luck, magickal power, abundance

Oak: Magickal power, fertility, strength, protection, luck, love, solar energies, courage, vitality

Flowers

Marigold: Solar energies, psychic power, magickal power, luck, protection, abundance, fertility, vitality

Sunflower: Solar energies, joy, peace, friendship, cooperation

Poppy: Psychic insight, magickal power, protection, dream magick, luck, spirit communication

Rose: Love, defense, magickal power, protection, binding

Aster: Love, luck, hope, friendship, psychic power

Cornflower: Fertility, abundance, psychic power, friendship, peace, luck

Crystals and Stones

Citrine: Solar energies, joy, strength, vitality, purification

Topaz: Calming, clear vision, psychic insight, trust

Carnelian: Strength, love, courage, calming, healing

Onyx: Protection, defense, binding, determination

Quartz: Psychic power, magickal power, luck, growth

Metals

Gold: Success, protection, wealth, health, lust, passion, courage, strength, solar energies

Brass: Solar energies, protection, prosperity, healing

Animals, Totems, Mythical Creatures

Lion: Strength, victory, courage, determination, defense, protection, physical power, success

Stag: Solar energies, earth energies, personal magnetism, fertility, abundance, strength

Eagle: Clarity, wisdom, energy, justice, strength, mental and spiritual power

Dog: Friendship, tenacity, community, keeper of the underworld

Squirrel: Earth energies, fertility, abundance, love, luck

Scents for Oils, Incense, Potpourri, or Just Floating in the Air

Cinnamon, apple, blackberry, marigold, patchouli

Tarot Keys

Strength, The Sun, Seven of Pentacles, Ten of Pentacles, Four of Wands, Justice, Wheel of Fortune

Symbols and Tools

Corn dolly: Harvested crops
Rowan cross: Solar energies, luck, protection
Cornucopia: Abundance, the harvest
Pentacle: Earth energies, prosperity, protection

Foods

Apples, corn, bread, squash, grains, nuts, berries, potatoes

Drinks

Wine, mead, apple cider

Activities and Traditions of Practice

Community fairs, reunions, gatherings, feasting, harvesting crops or wild herbs, making offerings to gods and ancestors, communicating with the dead, reflection and introspection, abundance magick, protection magick, sacrifice, games, competitions, expressing gratitude, celebrating success

Acts of Service
Sharing food and other necessities with those in need, sprucing up neglected cemeteries, offering your time and energy to help another person ease their burdens or lighten their workload, helping out at a community garden, doing yard work for elderly neighbors, providing social opportunities for those who are lonely or isolated

Alternative Names for Lughnasadh in Other Pagan Traditions
Lugnasadh (Irish Gaelic "Assembly of Lugh")
Bron-Trogain (Irish Gaelic "Bringing forth [the fruits of] the earth")
Lunasda (Scots Gaelic)
Lúnasa (Irish Gaelic)
Lunasdal (Scots Gaelic)
Luanistyn (Manx Gaelic)
Gwyl Awst (Welsh "Feast of Augustus")
Lammas (English "Loaf mass")
Hlafmaess (Anglo-Saxon "Loaf mass")

Freyfaxi (Heathen)

Hlafmaest (Norse)

Holidays or Traditions Occurring During the Lughnasadh Season in the Northern Hemisphere

RELIGIOUS

Ghost Festival (Chinese, August, variable dates according to lunar calendar)

Festival of the Dryads (Grecian, August 1–3)

Nemoralia (Roman, August 13–15)

Lammas (Anglo-Saxon, August 1)

Tisha B'Av (Jewish, July or August, variable dates according to the lunar calendar)

Assumption Day (Christian, August 15)

SECULAR

National Aviation Day (United States, August 19)

Senior Citizens Day (United States, August 21)

Holidays or Traditions Occurring during the Lughnasadh Season in the Southern Hemisphere

RELIGIOUS

Feast Day of Saint Brigit of Kildare (Catholic, February 1)

Candlemas, a.k.a The Presentation of Jesus at the Temple (Catholic, February 2)

Celebration of Yemanja (Candomblé, Brazil, February 2)

Nirvana Day (Mahayana Buddhist, February 8 or 15)
Lupercalia/Pan's Day (February 15)

SECULAR
Australia Day (Australia, January 26)
International Holocaust Remembrance Day (January 27)
World Wetlands Day (international, February 2)
Valentine's Day (February 14)
Chinese New Year (varies, late January to mid-February)

BIBLIOGRAPHY

"About Timoleague, West Cork." http://www.timoleague.ie/.

Addis, William E. and Thomas Arnold. *A Catholic Dictionary*. 1884. Reprint, Google Books, 2007.

ADF.org. "Lughnassadh Rituals." Accessed March 14, 2014, https://www.adf.org/rituals/celtic/lughnassadh.

Artisson, Robin. "The Differences in Traditional Witchcraft and Neo-Pagan Witchcraft, or Wicca." Accessed March 20,

2014, http://www.paganlore.com/witchcraft_vs_wicca.
aspx.

Asatru Alliance. "Runic Era Calendar." Accessed December
20, 2013, http://www.asatru.org/holidays.php.

Associated Newspapers, Ltd. *The Complete Book of Fortune*.
1936. Reprint. New York: Crescent Books, 1990.

Austin, Alfredo Lopez and Leonardo Lopez Lujan. *Mexico's
Indigenous Past*. 1996. Reprint, English translation, Bernard
R. Ortiz de Montellano, translator. Norman, OK: University of Oklahoma Press, 2001.

BeliefNet. "Celebrating First Harvest."Accessed March 1,
2014, http://www.beliefnet.com/Faiths/Pagan-and-Earth-
Based/2001/08/Celebrating-First-Harvest.aspx.

Biblehub.com. "Matthew 26:26." Accessed March 1, 2014,
http://biblehub.com/matthew/26-26.htm.

Binney, Ruth. *Wise Words and Country Ways: Weather Lore*.
Chapter 6, "Feast and Festival." New York: F & W Media,
Inc., 2012.

Buckland, Raymond: *Buckland's Book of Saxon Witchcraft*. York
Beach, ME: Weiser, 2005.

Calendar Customs. "Eastbourne Lammas Festival." Accessed
March 20, 2014, http://calendarcustoms.com/articles/
eastbourne-lammas-festival/.

Carmicheal, Alexander. *Carmina Gadelica: Hymns and
Incantations, Volume 1*. Edinburgh, UK: T. and A. Constable.

Accessed January 15, 2014, http://www.sacred-texts.com/neu/celt/cg1/cg1083.htm#page_198.

Circle Sanctuary. "Green Spirit 2014." Accessed March 20, 2014, https://www.circlesanctuary.org/index.php/our-events/festivals/green-spirit.

Conway, D. J. *Moon Magick*. St. Paul, MN: Llewellyn Publications, 1995.

Cooke, Michelle. "The Green Corn Ceremony of the Southeastern Indians." *The Journal of Chickasaw History and Culture*, Volume 14, no. 3, Spring 2013.

Craigie, Sir William Alexander. *The Religion of Ancient Scandinavia*. London: Archibald, Constable and Co., 1906.

Cunningham, Scott. *Cunningham's Encyclopedia of Wicca in the Kitchen*. 1990. Reprint, third edition, St. Paul, MN: Llewellyn Publications, 2003.

Cunningham, Scott. *The Complete Book of Incense, Oils, and Brews*. St. Paul, MN: Llewellyn Publications, 1996.

Cybercauldron. "Lughnasadh and Lammas." Accessed March 20, 2014, http://www.cybercauldron.co.uk/lughnasadh-and-lammas.

DragonOak. "Magical Properties of Wood and Tree Magic." Wiccan Altar. May 29, 2011. Accessed March 1, 2014, http://www.wiccanaltar.info/Magical-Properties-of-Wood-and-Magic-Trees.html.

Dunwoody, H. H. C. *Weather Proverbs*. United States of America, War Department, Signal Service Notes, Number

IX. Washington, DC: Government Printing Office, 1833.
Reprint, Google Books, 2009.

"Eastbourne Lammas Festival." Accessed March 20, 2014,
http://www.lammasfest.org/.

Eaton, William M. *Odyssey of the Pueblo Indians: An
Introduction to Pueblo Indian Petroglyphs, Pictographs, and Kiva
Art Murals in the Southwest.* Paducah, KY: Turner Publishing
Company, 1999.

Fife Council. "Lammas Market." Accessed March 20,
2014, http://www.fife.gov.uk/whatson/index.
cfm?fuseaction=whatson.display&id=625DA901-B029-
DDC2-C92E6087972CFE1F.

Futrell, Alison. *Blood in the Arena: The Spectacle of Roman
Power.* Austin, TX: University of Texas Press, 1997.

Gemstone Diva. "Healing and Magickal Properties of
Metals." Accessed March 20, 2014, http://www.gem-
stonedeva.com/metals.php.

Gomme, G. Lawerence. "Lammas Tide." *The Antiquary*, Volume VI, August, 1882. Reprint, Google Books, 2006.

Groom, Nick. *The Seasons: An Elegy for the Passing of the Year.*
London: Atlantic Books, 2013.

Guthrie, Ellen Emma. *Old Scottish Customs, Local and General.*
London: Hamilton, Adams, and Co., 1885. Reprint, Google
Books, 2007.

Harmony Tribe. "Sacred Harvest Festival." Accessed March 20, 2014, http://harmonytribe.org/content/sacred-harvest-festival.

Harvestfestivals.net. ""Harvest Festivals from Around the World." "Native American Harvest Festival."Accessed March 14th, 2014, http://www.harvestfestivals.net/nativeamericanfestivals.htm.

Heathen Temple. "It Is Freyfaxi to Some." Accessed March 1, 2014, http://heathentemple.tumblr.com/post/28501225871/it-is-freyfaxi-to-some.

Horne, Thomas Hartwell. *An Introduction to the Critical Study and Knowledge of the Holy Scriptures, volume III.* London: Longmans, Green, and Co., 1872. Reprint, Google Books, 2007.

Hutton, Ronald. *The Stations of the Sun: A History of the Ritual Year in Britain.* New York: Oxford University Press, 1996.

IITA: Research to Nourish Africa, R4D Review. "Yam Festival." April 8, 2010. Accessed February 5, 2014, http://r4dreview.org/2010/04/yam-festival/.

Iowa Lammasfest. Accessed March 20, 2014, http://www.lammasfest.us/home.php.

Ivanits, Linda J. *Russian Folk Beliefs.* 1989. Reprint, New York: M.E. Sharpe, 1992.

Joyce, Patrick Weston. *A Social History of Ancient Ireland, Volume II.* London, New York, and Bombay: Longmans, Green, and Company, 1903.

Knowlson, T. Sharper. *The Origins of Popular Superstitions and Customs*. Chapter 21 "Lammas Day."London: T. Werner Laurie Ltd., 1910, Accessed February 14, 2014, http://www.sacred-texts.com/neu/eng/osc/osc24.htm.

Lamont-Brown, Raymond and Frank G. Riddell. A (Very) Brief History of St. Andrews." Accessed March 20, 2014, http://www.saint-andrews.co.uk/CC/History.htm

Lipkowitz, Ina. *Words to Eat By: Five Foods and the Culinary History of the English Language*. New York: St. Martin's Press, 2011.

MacNeill, Mary. *The Festival of Lughnasa*. London: Oxford University Press, 1962.

Mazama, Ama. "Harvest Festivals." *Encyclopedia of African Religion, Volume 1*. Molefi Kete Asante and Ama Mazama, Editors. Thousand Oaks, CA: Sage Publications, Inc., 2009.

O'Curry, Eugene and William Kirby Sullivan, PhD, editor. *On the Manners and Customs of the Ancient Irish: A Series of Lectures by the Late Eugene O'Curry*. 1873. Reprint. Google Books.

Petch, Alison. "Harvest Trophies." England: The Other Within. Accessed March 30, 2014, http://england.prm.ox.ac.uk/englishness-harvest-trophies.html.

Pruen, Thomas. *An Illustration of the Liturgy of the Church of England*. London: Rivington, 1820. Reprint, Google Books, 2011.

Rainbow Gryphon. "Lughnasadh/Lammas." Accessed March 11, 2014, http://www.rainbowgryphon.com/spirituality/lughnasadh-lammas/.

Rhys, Sir John. "All Around the Wreckin."*Y Cymmrodor, Volume XXI.* London: Society of Cymmrodorion, 1908. Accessed March 14, 2014, https://archive.org/details/ycymmrodor-21cymmuoft.

Roy, Christian. *Traditional Festivals: A Multicultural Encyclopedia, Volume I.* Santa Barbara, CA: ABC-CLIO, Inc., 2005.

Santo Domingo Pueblo. "Feast Day." Accessed March 20, 2014, http://www.santodomingotribe.com/feastday-3/.

Shannon Heritage. "Lughnasa Festival." Accessed March 20, 2014, http://www.shannonheritage.com/Events/AnnualEvents/LughnasaFestival/.

"St. Andrews Merchants Association Chief Says Lammas Market May Have to Move." *The Courier*, 15 August 15, 2012. Accessed March 20, 2014, http://www.thecourier.co.uk/news/local/fife/st-andrews-merchants-association-chief-says-lammas-market-may-have-to-move-1.36261.

Swainson, Charles. *A Handbook of Weather Folk-lore.* Edinburgh, London: William Blackwood and Sons, 1873. Reprint, Google Books, 2009.

Takács, Sarolta A. *Vestal Virgins, Sibyls, and Matrons: Women in Roman Religion.* Austin, TX: University of Texas Press, 2008.

Talcroft, Barbara L. *Death of the Corn King: King and Goddess in Rosemary Sutcliff's Historical Fiction for Young Adults.* Metuchen and London: The Scarecrow Press, Inc., 1995.

The CR FAQ. "What do you do for Lunasa?" Accessed March 1, 2014, http://www.paganachd.com/faq/ritual.html#lunasa.

The Frank C. Brown Collection of North Carolina Folklore. *Volume VII: Popular Beliefs and Superstitions from North Carolina, Part 2.* Durham, NC: Duke University Press, 1964.

The Magickal Cat. "Herbal Grimoire." Accessed March 1, 2014, http://www.themagickalcat.com/Articles.asp?ID=242.

Theoi Greek Mythology. "Dryads and Oreiades." Accessed March 20, 2014, http://www.theoi.com/Nymphe/Dryads.html.

The Pagan Journey. "Lughnasadh." Accessed April 2, 2014, http://thepaganjourney.weebly.com/lughnasadh-aug-1july-31.html.

Thompson, Chris. "Notes on the Festival of Lughnasagh." Story Archeology. Accessed January 16, 2014, http://storyarchaeology.com/2012/12/10/notes-on-the-festival-of-lughnasagh/.

TimeandDate.com. "Holidays and Observances in United States in 2014." Accessed March 20, 2014, http://www.timeanddate.com/holidays/us/.

Town and Country Gardens. "August Weather Lore." Accessed March 20, 2014, http://townandcountrygardens. blogspot.com/2008/01/august-weather-lore.html.

Traditionalwitch.net. "Lughnasadh," Accessed March 14, 2014, http://www.traditionalwitch.net/_/esoterica/festivals-sabbats/lughnasadh-r34.

"Tullamore Show." Accessed March 20, 2014,http://tullamoreshow.com/.

Visit Eastbourne. "Lammas Festival at Western Lawns." Accessed March 20, 2014, http://www.visiteastbourne.com/ Eastbourne-Lammas-Festival/details/?dms=3&feature=1 &venue=3414532.

WGNS Radio. "Folklore Winter Forecast." March 1, 2012. Accessed March 20, 2014, http://wgnsradio.com/2011-2012-folklore-winter-forecast-cms-4009.

Wicca Spirituality. "Lammas: Divine Teamwork." Accessed March 1, 2014, http://www.wicca-spirituality.com/lammas-1.html.

Witch in the Valley. "Happy Lughnasadh!" Accessed March 20, 2014, http://witchinthevalley.com/2013/08/01/happy-lughnasadh/.

FURTHER READING

Blake, Deborah. *Everyday Witch Book of Rituals*. Woodbury, MN: Llewellyn, 2012.

Cunningham, Scott. *Living Wicca: A Further Guide for the Solitary Practioner*. St. Paul, MN: Llewellyn, 1993.

Dugan, Ellen. *Seasons of Witchery: Celebrating the Sabbats with the Garden Witch*. Woodbury, MN: Llewellyn, 2012.

Frazer, Sir James George. *The Golden Bough*. 1922. Reprint, New York: Bartleby.com, 2000. Accessed December 20, 2013, http://www.bartleby.com/196/.

Hutton, Ronald. *The Stations of the Sun: A History of the Ritual Year in Britain*. New York: Oxford University Press, 1996.

Hyde, Douglas. *A Literary History of Ireland from Earliest Times to the Present Day*. 1906. Reprint, Google ebooks, 2010.

Llewellyn. *Llewellyn's 2009–2010 Sabbats Almanac*. Woodbury: Llewellyn Worldwide, 2009.

———. *Llewellyn's 2010–2011 Sabbats Almanac*. Woodbury, MN: Llewellyn Worldwide, 2010.

———. *Llewellyn's 2011–2012 Sabbats Almanac*. Woodbury, MN: Llewellyn Worldwide, 2012.

———. *Llewellyn's 2012–2013 Sabbats Almanac*. Woodbury, MN: Llewellyn Worldwide, 2012.

———. *Llewellyn's 2013–2014 Sabbats Almanac*. Woodbury, MN: Llewellyn Worldwide, 2013.

MacLeod, Sharon Paice. *Celtic Myth and Religion: A Study of Traditional Belief, with Newly Translated Prayers, Poems, and Songs*. Jefferson, MO: McFarland and Company, 2012.

INDEX

A

Abundance, 21, 22, 33, 34, 43, 52, 53, 124, 138, 142, 177, 181–185

Acorn, 82

Ale, 26, 27, 151, 156

Ancestors, 7, 8, 32, 42, 43, 48, 62, 178, 184

Anglo-Saxon, 22, 23, 29, 50, 185, 186

Apple, 33, 79, 96, 105–108, 111, 121, 122, 144, 157–159, 162–164, 182, 184

Apple Savior, 33

Asatru, 48
August Eve, 47

B
Berries, 44–47, 114-116, 178, 184
Bilberries, 16, 95, 115
Blackberries, 47, 63, 115
Blueberries, 46, 95, 115, 125
Bonnach Lunastain, 24
Bread, 7, 23, 35–37, 44, 45, 47, 50, 65, 66, 96,
    109, 110, 124, 142, 151, 171–173, 184
Bron-trogain, 22, 185
Bull, 16
Byzantine Empire, 35

C
Cailleachan, 47
Camping, 54, 88
Carman, 19, 20
Cattle, 21, 24, 76
Celtic, 7, 8, 15, 16, 22–24, 30, 31, 46, 47, 49,
    50, 121, 156, 180
Celtic Reconstructionist, 46
Cherokee, 31

Chickasaw, 31

Choctaw, 31

Christianity, 23, 24, 36, 48

Communion, 36, 37

Consualia, 33

Consus, 33, 180

Contracts, 50

Country Fair, 44, 53, 56–57, 121

Corn, 21, 26, 27, 30, 31, 35, 36, 51, 52, 55, 56,
    85, 86, 95, 96, 99, 106, 112–114, 117–119,
    125, 127, 150–152, 184

Corn Divination, 85, 86

Corn Dollies, 27, 52

Corn King, 52

Creek, 31

Crops, 6, 7, 24, 29, 36, 42, 44, 49, 53, 59, 71,
    90, 91, 99, 164–168, 171, 173, 178, 184

Cross-quarter Days, 5, 8, 50

D

Dancing, 21, 30, 32, 45, 51, 52, 53, 55, 57,
    156

Danu, 16, 43, 137–139, 180

Dead, 36, 43, 61, 62, 178, 182, 184

Death, 37, 43, 48, 51, 62, 63, 99, 100,
    177
Druid (Modern), 49–50

E
Eastbourne Lammas Festival, 58, 59
Eclectic Witchcraft, 52
England, 15, 27, 29, 58, 85, 117
Eucharist, 36

F
Family-friendly Events, 45, 46, 47, 53–54,
    54–55, 58
Fair of Tailteann, 18, 19
Fairs, 19–21, 24, 30, 44, 184
Feasting, 16, 18, 21, 24, 43-45, 52, 53, 61,
    65, 184
Feast of First Fruits, 23
Fertility, 6, 16, 22, 30, 31, 43, 48, 112,
    143, 153, 181–183
First fruits, 15, 21-23, 33, 35, 37, 44, 47, 121
Frey, 48
Freyfaxi, 48, 186

G

Ga, 32

Games, 7, 17, 18, 21, 30, 47, 53, 66, 67,
   156, 185

Ghana, 32

Gratitude, 7, 31, 37, 42, 43, 44, 52, 56, 91, 79,
   95, 101, 104, 107, 122–125, 140–141, 149,
   150–156, 172–174, 177, 185

Gravesites,18, 19, 62

Green Corn Festival, 31

Green Spirit Festival, 53, 54

Growing Moon Dance, 30

Gwyl Awst, 15, 30, 185

H

Handfasting, 19, 50

Heathen, 48, 186

Hlafmaesse, 15, 22, 23

Holly King, 5, 7

Homowo Festival, 32

Honey Savior, 33

Hopi, 30, 31

Horses, 18, 21, 57, 76

I

Ibo, 32

Iowa Lammasfest, 54

Ireland, 15, 17-20, 22, 29, 56–59,
    156

Isle of Man, 15

J

Jewish, 35, 186

K

Kirn Babies, 27

L

Lá Lúnasa, 46, 47

Lammas, 7, 9, 15, 23-27, 29, 47, 50, 51, 53,
    54, 58, 59, 85, 178, 185, 186

Lammas bannock, 24

Lammas lands, 29

Livestock, 6, 7, 20, 24, 25, 27, 57, 76, 90,
    91, 117

Loaf Mass, 22, 185

Love, 37, 73, 79, 90, 106, 107, 111, 115, 116,
    123, 124, 153, 154, 161, 166, 170, 174,
    181–183

Lugh, 15-18, 30, 43, 47, 49, 62, 83, 121, 133–136, 156, 164, 166, 180, 185

Lunasda, 15, 185

M

March Stones, 28

Marua Dance, 30

Mead, 151, 184

Mercury, 16

N

Neopagan, 5, 7, 48, 51

New Yam Festival, 32

Nigeria, 32

Norse, 181, 186

Nut Savior, 33

Nymphs, 43, 144, 145, 179

O

Oak King, 5, 7

Oaths, 50, 171

Old Style Lammas, 15, 178

Olive crown, 36

Ops, 33, 143, 180

Ox, 36

P

Pacts, 50, 171

Pendulum, 90, 91

Peter's Pence, 29

Picnics, 30, 43, 52, 53

Potatoes, 17, 44, 79–80, 97, 184

Property, 24, 27, 29, 91, 117, 120, 128

Prosperity, 21, 52, 71, 76, 79–82, 84, 112, 115, 116, 177, 181–184

Protection, 6, 21, 23, 24, 43, 47, 49, 52, 76, 90, 91, 115–117, 120, 136, 144, 149, 164, 170, 177, 181–185

R

Radbod, 48

Riding of the Marches, 27

Rome, 29, 34, 35

Roman, 16, 33, 34, 180, 181, 186

Rowan Cross, 184

Russia, 33

S

Sacred Harvest Festival, 54

Sacrifice, 7, 16, 31, 36, 37, 44, 48, 52, 53, 61, 99, 122, 149, 151, 153, 156, 177, 185

Saint Dominic, 55

Saint Peter in Chains, 35

Santo Domingo, 55–56

Scotland, 15, 18, 25–27, 29, 59,
    85

Scrying, 87, 89, 90

Seonaidh, 26, 27

Singing, 30, 32, 51, 52, 124

Snake Dance, 31

Spear of Victory, 49

Spirit of Vegetation, 149, 152, 154–156,
    179

Stikklestad Day, 48

T

Tailtiu, 18, 19, 46, 133, 136, 156,
    180

Talisman, 80-84

Telltown marriages, 19

Timoleague Festival, 58

Tower, 25, 26

Traditional Witchcraft, 50

Tree, 64, 128, 179

Tuatha de Danaan, 16, 18

Tullamore Show, 56, 57

U

United States, 30, 46, 85, 186

V

Victoria Virgo, 33

Victory, 16, 33, 34, 49, 139, 182, 183

W

Wales, 15, 30

Weather, 30, 84, 85

West Africa, 32

Wet Savior, 33

Wheel of the Year, 1–4, 8, 9, 11, 15, 47

Wiccan, 5, 6, 8, 47, 49, 52, 53

Wild-harvested Foods, 43, 44, 46, 50, 53, 63,
      178, 184

Y

Yoruba, 32

About the Author

Melanie Marquis is a lifelong practitioner of magick, founder of the United Witches global coven, and organizer of Denver Pagans. She has written for the American Tarot Association, Llewellyn's almanacs and datebooks, and national and international Pagan publications including *Circle* and *Pentacle Magazine*. She resides in Colorado. Visit her online at http://www.melaniemarquis.com.